D1621959

Your Social Media Job Search
Use LinkedIn, Twitter, and other tools to Get the Career You Want!

By Robert Hellmann, President of *Hellmann Career Consulting*,
www.hellmannconsulting.com

Published by:
Robert Hellmann LLC, New York, USA

THANK YOU FOR YOUR PURCHASE

Trademarks

The Five O'Clock Club® is a federally registered trademark of The Five O'Clock Club, Inc.
LinkedIn® is a federally registered trademark of LinkedIn, Ltd.
Twitter® is a federally registered trademark of Twitter, Inc.
Facebook® is a federally registered trademark of Facebook, Inc.
All terms mentioned in this book that are known to be trademarks or service marks have been appropriately capitalized. Use of a term in this book should not be regarded as affecting the validity of any Trademark or Service Mark.

Photos and Illustrations

Illustrations and photos on pages 11, 16, and 81 © 2010 JupiterImages Corporation
All photos and images on the cover, the photo on page 9 and the illustration on page 77 are licensed through istockphoto, www.istockphoto.com
Photos on pages 63 and 84 © 2010 by Robert Hellmann

Limit of Liability/Disclaimer of Warranty:

This eBook is sold with the following understanding:
While the publisher and author have used their best efforts in preparing this eBook, they make no representations or warranties with respect to the accuracy or completeness of the contents of this eBook and specifically disclaim any implied warranties of merchantability or fitness for a particular purpose. No warranty may be created or extended by sales representatives or written sales materials. The advice and strategies contained herein may not be suitable for your situation. Neither the publisher nor author shall be liable for any damages arising herefrom. The fact that an organization or website is referred to in this work as a citation and/or a potential source of further information does not meant that the author endorses the information the organization or website may provide or recommendations it may make. Further, readers should be aware that internet websites listed in this work may have changed or disappeared between when this work was written and when it is read.

TABLE OF CONTENTS

About the Author 5

Note to the Reader About this Edition 7

How to Read this Book 8

Introduction 10

1. Social Media's Priority in A Job Search 12

How to Prioritize 12
Follow These Steps 12

2. LinkedIn.. 17

What Is LinkedIn? 17

Why Use LinkedIn?.. 18

Getting Set-up on LinkedIn.................................. 20
LinkedIn Settings... 20
Creating a Powerful LinkedIn Profile 21
Building Your LinkedIn Network 31
Join LinkedIn Groups.. 35
Notating & "Tagging" Your Network.......................... 37

Using LinkedIn... 38
Career Research... 38
Find People in Companies/Industries........................ 44
How to Contact People that You Find........................ 48
Answering LinkedIn Ads...................................... 54
Keeping in Touch with Your Network......................... 54
If You're a Consultant or Own a Company.................... 56
Your "Company Page".. 56
LinkedIn On-the-Job 56

Additional Case Studies..................................... 59

LinkedIn's Paid Services.................................... 60

Common Concerns and Questions about LinkedIn 61
"My Boss Will Know I'm Looking" 61

"I don't want some people to know I'm changing my profile" 61
"I don't want all of my information out there for anyone to see" 62
"Shouldn't I only connect with people in my profession?" 62

3. Email Lists 64

4. Twitter 66

What Is Twitter? 66

Who should be on Twitter? 67

How Twitter Can Help Your Job Search 67

Getting Set-up on Twitter 68
Organizing Your Tweets using a "Dashboard" 70

Using Twitter 70
A Case Study 70

5. Blogs 78

What is a Blog? 78

Writing Your Own Blog 78

Reading Other People's Blogs 79
Keeping Track of the Blogs You Follow with "Feed Readers" 80

6. Facebook 82

Facebook Groups 83

Facebook Integration with www.Simplyhired.com 83

Facebook Pages 84

7. job search Case Study: Using Limited Time Wisely ... 85

8. Social Media for Building A Business 89

9. Cross-Platform Thoughts 95

Google Yourself 95

Mobile Applications ("Apps") 95

Appendix 1: Additional Resources..................................... 97

Appendix 2: Eight Rules For Writing Great Letters 99

Glossary of Terms 102

ABOUT THE AUTHOR

As President of *Hellmann Career Consulting*, Robert Hellmann provides a range of career services to individuals and organizations. He's a certified **Five O'Clock Club Career Coach** and an adjunct **Instructor at New York University**. He runs weekly groups for jobseekers nationally on behalf of the Club, and has served as a Club Vice President. Rob is also a **DOOR International** trainer, delivering career advancement seminars to multinational and Fortune 500 institutions.

Rob's background includes over 20 years of experience in Career Development, Organizational Development, and Marketing, with clients and employers including **American Express, JP Morgan Chase, the Federal Reserve Bank of New York**, and the **Audubon Society**. He has developed career services training programs for a number of organizations including **Columbia University, Fordham University, Montclair State University, Baruch College** and **Pace University**.

Rob's career-related insights and commentary have appeared in media outlets such as **the New York Times, Forbes, the Washington Post, Money Magazine, the Chicago Tribune, CNBC.com, NBC News** and **ABC News**.

Active in non-profit organizations, Rob has chaired the Career Development Committee for the New York chapter of the **Marketing Executives Networking Group (MENG)** and worked with the **Big Brother/Big Sister** program to offer career-related support.

As a coach, Rob combines his marketing background with his coaching training and experience to help clients successfully market themselves in their careers, and make the "right" career decisions. He has helped thousands of clients reach their job-search, career and on-the-job goals through his active private practice. Feel free to contact him at rob@hellmannconsulting.com, or visit his website at www.hellmannconsulting.com.

*"In 20 years you'll regret more the things you didn't do
than the ones you did."*
Mark Twain

This book is dedicated to
all those who seek to be the architects of their own destiny.

NOTE TO THE READER ABOUT THIS EDITION

Dear Reader,

This edition contains a significantly expanded LinkedIn chapter, based on client experiences and additional research conducted over the past year. LinkedIn has also undergone significant interface changes that required updating this text. Both the "Getting Set Up" and "Using LinkedIn" sections contain substantial new material.

While job-search remains a key focus in this edition, I made the content more relevant to those looking to advance their careers within their current job or organization. In particular, I have included a new section in the LinkedIn chapter on this topic. I have retained and re-edited the section on how to use social media applications to build your business.

I've also included a new item in the Appendix on how to write great emails and cover letters. So much of social media is about finding the right people to follow and contact. But not enough has been written on how specifically to reach out to them, so that you get the response you want.

As far as the social media applications covered in this book, they remain unchanged from the prior edition. Despite some newcomers that have received a substantial following and media attention (Pinterest, Foursquare, Google+), none have emerged that have a combination of both a large enough following and broad-based, "killer" job-search/career advancement features to receive attention in this book.

This book is also available in digital form as an eBook. Once you have purchased this paperback version, you can **download the latest version of the eBook for free** (it's updated as needed throughout the year). Just follow the instructions in the Appendix, on page 104 of this book.

If you have any comments or suggestions for future editions, or you want to share your results from using this guide, I would appreciate hearing from you at rob@hellmannconsulting.com.

Thanks for your interest in this book, and best wishes on reaching your goals!

Robert Hellman

HOW TO READ THIS BOOK

You can read this book in two ways-- either straight through, or selectively and out of order. For those preferring the latter approach, I've ranked below the importance of each section to your job search.

Required Reading: Sections 1 (Social Media's Priority...), 2 (LinkedIn) and 5 (blogs): Prioritizing the activities that take up your valuable job-search time and using LinkedIn's powerful features are essential to conducting an effective job search these days, and can be of great help overall in advancing your career. The short chapter on Blogs contains essential tips on how to set yourself up for ongoing research in your job target or area of specialization.

Highly Recommended: Section 3 (Email Lists): This short section is also universally relevant, as email lists can be very useful to a job search or career advancement.

Highly Recommended: Section 7 (Case Study: Using Limited Time Wisely): This section brings all of the social media applications in this book together in a job search case study. Reading this section will give you another perspective on how to prioritize all the work you need to do to have an effective search.

Highly Recommended: Appendix 2 (Writing Great Letters and Emails that Get Meetings): Enough said.

Optional: Section 4 (Twitter): You don't have to be on Twitter to have a good job search. It takes some time to set it up correctly and may or may not work well for your particular profession. The payoff with using Twitter for your search could potentially be very high, however, which is why I've devoted so much space to it. I suggest at least skimming the first couple of pages of this chapter so that you can make a well-informed decision on whether to explore Twitter further.

Optional: Section 6 (Facebook): How useful this application is to you will depend on your unique situation. Since the section is short, I would recommend reviewing it at some point. The information will help you to conduct a more productive job search.

Optional: Sections 8 (Social Media for Building your Business): For those of you who are considering starting a business or consulting practice, or are already in one, this section is for you.

INTRODUCTION

"If content is king, then conversation is queen."
John Munsell

This edition has been written during a time when a "buyer's market" still prevails in hiring. Gone are the days when simply responding to ads was enough to get a good job quickly, or just doing your job well was enough to keep it. Today, you need to know how to use every tool in your arsenal to land the job you want in a reasonable amount of time, and to keep or advance in the job you have.

In my practice coaching clients on their job searches and careers, new clients who haven't been using social media effectively (or at all) span generations. Often younger clients feel that Facebook alone is enough (it's not) while more seasoned clients are put off by the learning curve. Even those comfortable using these applications are often unaware of powerful career advancement features. I share this book with career-advancers of all ages so they know how to boost their effectiveness using social media to land jobs, clients, careers, or promotions— putting them ahead of their less social-media savvy competition.

To begin, let's define **social media**: It's primarily online or mobile media that enables conversation and interaction between people.

Why should you read this book?

This guide stems from my work as a career coach with an active practice. I bring insights based on daily experience with powerful techniques that will help you get the job and career you want.

My recommendations incorporate learning from my own research and from client experiences. They also incorporate a highly effective, research-based approach to the job search: the *Five O'Clock Club* career advancement methodology (see Appendix for more information). I'm certified in this methodology, and have leveraged it in helping thousands of clients land jobs and advance in their careers.

This book also highlights **when you should incorporate specific applications**. For some it can be tempting to jump right on the social media bandwagon with wild abandon. But since you are on a mission to get the job, clients or career you want, you need to take a more thoughtful approach. This book shows you how to prioritize the use of individual social media applications within your overall effort, so you don't waste time, and **use your**

precious time productively.

As layoffs have become more routine, I've seen more jobseekers look into starting their own business or consulting practice, as a route to improved income security. This edition includes a chapter on how to **leverage social media to get more clients and customers**.

Lastly, I've shared **client examples and case studies** throughout. Much of this book involves step-by-step "how-to" instructions. Reviewing the experiences of clients who've followed these steps should make this approach come alive for you.

What Social Media Applications Will be Covered, and Why?

Social media has a lot of buzz: What is all this twitter about Twitter? Do I really need to link-up with LinkedIn or face Facebook? In selecting applications to review, I considered: 1) whether helpful career advancement features are free to use, 2) how useful these features are, 3) the number of users, and 4) the amount of media attention. These factors led me to focus on five applications:

LinkedIn: is a thoroughly proven job search/career management aid. If your job targets or clients are well represented on LinkedIn, you should be active on this platform.

Email Lists: are an often-overlooked, "low-tech" social networking tool. Yet they have shown great results and are widely accessible.

Twitter: has received a lot of press and has many users, including leaders in a variety of professions. It may have potential to enhance your job search or career, depending on your profession.

Facebook: With over a billion users, Facebook is just too large for it not to be evaluated.

Blogs: are easy to access and use, and have potential as a job-search aid in many situations.

On another note, I excluded platforms that, although in many cases very popular and frequently mentioned in the media, just don't yet have the usage volume, the career-oriented "culture," or the broad-based practical career applications to be included. These platforms include Google+, Pinterest, Foursquare, and a host of smaller applications.

Early form of Social Media

1. SOCIAL MEDIA'S PRIORITY IN A JOB SEARCH

"Lost time is never found again."
Proverb

How to Prioritize

Any social activity that you participate in has the potential to help you get interviews, but obviously, some are far more effective than others. One client was spending much of his job-search time going to regular networking meetings at an association where most of the people showing up were unemployed competitors for jobs in his field! It took him about two hours of commuting time to get to and from these meetings. After three months with no success, he came to me, and we mapped out more effective ways for him to spend his valuable job-search time.

A golden rule: *pick the low-hanging fruit first.* That is, do the easy things that are likely to get great results quickly before tackling the harder things.[1] Go for the biggest bang for the buck first. For example, what is the easiest way to research a person or company? Do a Google search to see what comes up, visit the company's website and poke around, or check out their LinkedIn profiles!

Also, think about how you can tap into the so-called "hidden job market" via networking and building new relationships. You want to **prioritize efforts that will enable you to bypass the glut of applicants going through ads or recruiting firms**, as well as land interviews for positions that may not be advertised (or that you help to create). Most of my clients are getting interviews these days by both reaching out to their network and building new relationships with people who can help them (and not via answering ads and contacting recruiting firms). You should prioritize your efforts as well.

Follow These Steps

The sequence of job search steps below will show you how the social media

---

[1] "Pareto Optimality," or the "80/20 rule," is the same idea (Google it, you will see pages of info). That is, we spend 20% of our time doing 80% of the work, and 80% of our time doing the remaining 20%. Focus your efforts on the 80% that takes only 20% of your time to do. A related concept: "the perfect is the enemy of the good."

applications covered in this book should fit into your larger job search. Feel free to adjust the recommended order for your unique situation.

1) **Research potential professions and industries**

Use research to help you select the right positions to go for, or to ensure that you will be able to speak the language of your target audience. Some clients come to me after getting no results with their resume. Often, the problem is either that they are speaking the jargon of their last employer instead of their future one, or they don't have a clear job target and thus aren't speaking to any particular audience. Research is key to addressing these issues. Do as much or as little research as you need to depending on where you are in your job search. Approach your research in the following order:

1. Start with the links on my website, www.hellmannconsulting.com , under "Industry and Occupational Research", to help you identify and speak to your target audience effectively.

2. Search online job boards (websites containing job ads) to see what types of jobs exist, and how employers describe them. Adopt the terminology and jargon in these descriptions when approaching a prospective employer in the same job-target (industry or profession). If you need a starting place, scroll down to the list of job boards on my website.

3. Do Google searches on the profession or industry you are targeting, and see what comes up, e.g., articles, blogs, online journals, etc.

4. Read the "Career Research" sub-section of the "LinkedIn" chapter in this book (see Table of Contents); LinkedIn has a host of valuable career, job target, people and company research capabilities.

5. Subscribe to online journals to easily search for information on your target-audience's needs.

6. Talk to people who are in the field you want to enter to gain their insight and advice. Learn how good a fit you are for your targets, and how you should market yourself.

   You can find people to talk to by:

   a. Joining professional or alumni associations, and using their online member database to contact members for informational meetings.

   b. Reaching out to people you already know, via email or a phone call.

   c. Searching for relevant discussions on email lists (read the "Email

<u>Lists</u>" chapter).

    d.   Asking questions and starting new discussions on these email lists.

    e.   Joining LinkedIn to ask questions of other members, read or participate in member discussions, and contact members for informational meetings.

    f.   Investigating whether Twitter can help you with additional target research (read the "<u>Twitter</u>" chapter).

2) Get the word out to your entire network about your search

The more people who know about your search, the more referrals you can get to people who may be in a position to hire you. Initially, you are building the wide end of your "getting interviews" pipeline, which you expect to lead to a far smaller number of conversations with people in a position to hire you. Here's the suggested sequence for making this happen:

1.   Get set up on LinkedIn if a lot of people in your industry or profession use it. Read the "<u>Find People in Companies/Industries</u>," "<u>How to Contact People</u>," and "<u>Keeping in Touch with Your Network</u>" subsections of the "LinkedIn" chapter.

2.   Make a list of your entire network (your dentist, family and friends, current and former co-workers, old professors— everyone you can think of) and let them know about your search. Contact them by the channel that is most likely to get a response, be it email, Facebook, LinkedIn, or by tweeting your followers (see the <u>Twitter</u> chapter). A good rule of thumb is to aim for 200 people.

3) Set yourself up for maintaining momentum in your search

That is, get set up for conducting ongoing job-related research, pursuing new networking opportunities, and building helpful relationships with people whom you don't know.

1.   Join associations (including professional, industry, and alumni associations).

2.   Similarly, join LinkedIn groups (read the "<u>Join LinkedIn Groups</u>" subsection of the LinkedIn chapter).

3.   Set up "*LinkedIn Today*" to receive timely posts about developments in your industry/profession (see the "<u>Researching Career Options</u>" subsection of the LinkedIn chapter).

4. Subscribe to the appropriate journals that will allow you to keep abreast of the latest developments in your field and identify people to contact. I prefer online journals because they are easier to search for the information you want.

5. Subscribe to blogs (see the "Blogs" chapter) that you find through referrals or articles you've read, to keep updated on both leaders in your field and developments in your job target.

6. Set up Google Alerts that enable you to keep on top of news regarding organizations that are of interest to you.[2]

7. Join email lists that are relevant to your job target.

8. Explore whether Twitter will benefit your target research and help build new interview-generating relationships. If so, then get set up properly on Twitter.

4) Ongoing Actions to Build and Maintain Momentum
Once you have set yourself up for a productive search, take these actions.

1. Build your LinkedIn network (read the "Building Your LinkedIn Network" subsection of the LinkedIn chapter).

2. Get introductions to people via your LinkedIn network (read the "How to Contact People that You Find" subsection of the LinkedIn chapter).

3. Remind your network of your search at least once a month, via the most appropriate channel, e.g. email, LinkedIn, Facebook, Twitter, etc. (your update frequency will vary depending on the channel).

4. Contact people directly who you don't know using your associations' online databases or LinkedIn groups.

5. Read or participate in online conversations via LinkedIn or email lists you belong to (see the "Email Lists" chapter).

6. If Twitter works for your job target, briefly (15 minutes) review your Twitter "feeds" every one to three days to keep current with the latest news, and spot opportunities for new relationship-building.

---

[2] For Google alerts, here's what you do: 1) Go to news.google.com. 2) Type in search terms for a company you are interested in. 3) Once you like the results you are getting from the search terms, scroll down and click on "Create an email alert for <company name>."

5) Longer term, if the "low hanging fruit" from the steps above has all been picked:

1. Add to the comments on the blogs of leaders in your field who might be helpful in getting you interviews or informational meetings.
2. Similarly, comment on the tweets of leaders in your field who you are following and seek to establish a dialogue that could lead to referrals/interviews (see the "Twitter" chapter).
3. If you are already on Facebook, explore Facebook "Groups" to see if any are worth joining (see the "Facebook" chapter).
4. If you feel the need to show that you are current in your field, consider starting your own blog (see the "Blogs" chapter).

OK, now put on your social media swimsuit, and let's dive in!

**The Next Step in
Social Media's Evolution**

2. LINKEDIN

*"**Six degrees of separation** refers to the idea that everyone is at most six steps away from any other person on Earth…"* (**Wikipedia**)

In this Chapter:

✓ For most professionals, LinkedIn is a MUST for a job search or career networking.

✓ Take advantage of LinkedIn's unique features that make it easier to get meetings.

   ❖ Get introductions through your LinkedIn Network.

   ❖ Contact people you don't know via LinkedIn Groups.

   ❖ Easily keep in touch with your network.

   ❖ Demonstrate your expertise to potential employers via a powerful LinkedIn Profile.

   ❖ Find hiring managers for ads posted on LinkedIn and contact them directly.

   ❖ Maintain your presence in a place that recruiters use to search for candidates.

   ❖ Research companies, industries, professions, and skills.

What Is LinkedIn?

LinkedIn, accessed at www.linkedin.com, enables users to keep in touch with and expand their professional networks, get introductions to others outside their immediate network, and join groups of professionals organized around industries, professions, and associations.

The "culture" of LinkedIn is all about advancing your professional career. With a global membership of over 200 million, the site is well designed to make it easy to develop and maintain professional relationships. Both in-house recruiters and recruiting firms are using LinkedIn to scan profiles for viable candidates.

LinkedIn has been useful to jobseekers and career advancers at all levels. One client in business development had been very successful at getting both informational meetings and interviews by using LinkedIn for networking and contacting people he didn't know—on average about one interview a week over a two month period![3] He used LinkedIn Groups to find people to contact. (I'll review Groups in a later section.) These positive results are typical for clients using LinkedIn.

Why Use LinkedIn?

Throughout your search, you want to have a presence in places where you can connect with people who can help you. LinkedIn is such a place. Use it to connect to people who can hire you, refer you, or provide information about your job target. LinkedIn tends to attract those whose professions are characterized by periodic job changes (including consultants) or entrepreneurs looking for an audience.

Although many professions are represented well on LinkedIn, those with very low job turnover have a smaller presence. Primary or secondary school teachers are an example. Conversations with colleagues in your job target (or quick searches on LinkedIn itself) can help you to decide whether to prioritize LinkedIn as a job search aid. In most cases, the answer will be "yes."

LinkedIn enables you to do the following easily and effectively:
- **Develop and maintain a network** of people who can help your career.
- **Get introductions** to people in organizations where you would like to work via your network.
- **Contact people whom you don't know** for information or meetings.
- **Research people, companies, industries and professions** to prepare for meetings or learn more about a job target.
- **Identify key hiring managers or influencers** at a company so that you can contact them. Finding these people, often a difficult part of the search, is made easier on LinkedIn.
- **Respond to ads** more effectively; bypass the glut of applications for a typical job posting.
- **Maintain a presence** in a location where **recruiters** search for qualified candidates. Your LinkedIn presence is also relevant for recruiters who use Google searches to source candidates, since your LinkedIn profile will show up in Google search results.

LinkedIn Terms
1st Degree Network: the people you connect with directly.

---

[3] We met to discuss how he could be more effective at turning interviews into offers.

2nd Degree Network: the people who connect directly with your 1st degree network.

3rd Degree Network: the people who connect directly with your 2nd degree network.

Group: LinkedIn members who congregate in an organized LinkedIn forum around a specific topic, profession, or association.

Your 1st degree network includes people who have accepted your invitation to connect, or sent you an invitation that you have accepted. Each person in your 1st degree network has his or her own 1st degree network, which becomes your 2nd degree network. Each person in your 2nd degree network has his or her own 1st degree network which becomes your 3rd degree network.

Your Network of Trusted Professionals

You are at the center of your network. Your connections can introduce you to 5,190,400+ professionals — here's how your network breaks down:

1	**Your Connections** Your trusted friends and colleagues	381
2	**Two degrees away** Friends of friends; each connected to one of your connections	116,600+
3	**Three degrees away** Reach these users through a friend and one of their friends	5,073,400+
	Total users you can contact through an Introduction	5,190,400+

Your 1st degree network can introduce you to people in your 2nd degree network, and indirectly to people in your 3rd degree network. See the chart above for what my network looked like a while back. I had connected to 381 people directly, which theoretically enabled me to get introductions to almost 5.2 million people! But in reality, I actually have access to far more than 5.2 million people, because of the power of LinkedIn Groups; the reason is that in most cases, you can message anyone within a group that you share.

The sections that follow explain 1) how to get set up on LinkedIn, and then 2) how to contact people via either your network or "groups" and make use of other powerful features.

Getting Set-up on LinkedIn

Go to www.LinkedIn.com for your free log-on ID and password. Once you log in, follow the prompts to begin creating your profile and inviting people to connect with you.

Early on you will be prompted with options to build your network quickly by importing all of your contacts from your online or desktop address book, in order to send these contacts LinkedIn invitations. **I would advise skipping these steps for now.** You want to build a decent LinkedIn profile first before inviting people to connect with you.

When finished with these initial prompts, you will notice that you are on the Home page, as indicated by the highlighted word on the top menu. Click on the "Profile" menu option at the top of the page, then "Edit Profile," as pictured below. You are now ready to create your LinkedIn profile.

(**NOTE:** LinkedIn periodically modifies the menu structure. When that happens, it may take you an extra minute or two to find out where, for example, the "*Edit Profile*" menu option now resides. But rest assured, the functionality described in this book will be there! In the unlikely event that you get stuck, click on the tiny picture of you at the top right of the page, select "*Help*" and type your question, e.g. "How do I Edit Profile?" You will then see step-by-step instructions.)

LinkedIn Settings

Before you are going to write (or re-write) your profile, set your visibility settings so no one in your network will get notified of changes to your profile in their weekly network activity email. You don't want people to check out your profile when it's not ready! There's only one chance to make a good first impression. And, if you are connected to your boss, you may not want to spark her curiosity with a notification of changes to your profile.

To temporarily prevent your network from being notified of changes, go to the "Settings Page" (see below), click on "*Turn on/off your activity broadcasts*" and set it to "off." Once your profile is in reasonably good shape, go back to your settings and open them up for maximum visibility; if you are in a job search, you want to be found.

The "Settings" Page

The link to this page is located on the top right of your LinkedIn screen, by clicking on the little picture of you, and then selecting "Privacy & Settings." You should review this section and know what's in it, as you may want to change your settings regarding privacy, how and when you are contacted, your visibility on LinkedIn, and how you notify others of changes to your profile.

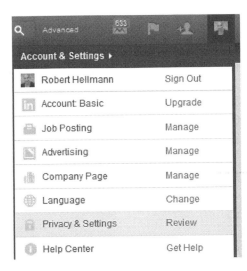

One setting you would want to change right away is: *Edit Public Profile Settings*. This section allows you to, among other things, select an easy-to-remember URL, by entering one under "Customize this Address." This friendlier URL can now be used in your resume or in your email signature. For example, originally, the link to my profile was something like: http://www.linkedin.com/pub/Robert-Hellmann/21/a8/244. I was able to change it to www.linkedin.com/in/roberthellmann.

Make your completed public profile as visible as you can. I recommend the default "Full View" once you feel your profile is in good shape. If you feel uncomfortable with this, you can alter details of what is visible in this section.

The rest of the settings are straightforward so you don't need me to walk you through it. I will, however, cover certain settings in later sections.

Creating a Powerful LinkedIn Profile

In most cases, create an effective profile by following the same principles that I would recommend for your resume, with a few exceptions (discussed below). In fact, I recommend cutting/pasting your well-crafted resume directly to the corresponding LinkedIn sections, assuming the exceptions below don't require you to significantly alter it. In particular,

- ✓ Write your profile (as you do your resume) for the specific audience that you want to reach, that is, the people who could hire you in your job target.
- ✓ Use the phrasing and keywords that will resonate with your target audience.
- ✓ Use clear, concise, to-the-point language. Although LinkedIn doesn't

easily give you a bullet-point option, you can use dashes or asterisks as a substitute, to help create a tight feel. You can also copy/paste bullet points from Microsoft Word into your profile.

✓ Make your profile accomplishment-oriented when appropriate; include the impact of what you did, not just your responsibilities. For example, say "increased sales by 23%" or "substantially improved efficiency." I tell clients to always seek to write accomplishment-oriented bullets.

✓ Your profile should not be a laundry list of everything you've done. Instead only include the experience that applies to your job target, and exclude or minimize experience that doesn't.

✓ Have a strong Summary Section, essentially your greatest hits or "pitch," at the top of your profile.

You can view your profile as others see it by selecting "Profile" on the top menu and then "View."

For additional guidance on writing profiles, see these examples, and the "Box" that follows:

- www.linkedin.com/in/roberthellmann (my profile)
- www.linkedin.com/in/michelecabay
- www.linkedin.com/in/ericweisburg

Differences between Resumes and Profiles

Keeping these four differences in mind as you adapt your resume to your profile may require you to make significant changes to your resume content, to make it work for your profile.

Only one Profile, so you need to choose

It is impractical and confusing to spread your network across multiple profiles (unlike your resume, where you can and should have a different resume for each job target). Having only one profile means that you will have to decide whether to go more general, to encompass multiple job targets, or to focus your profile on your primary job target only.

Your decision will depend on your specific situation. I recommend writing your profile for your primary job target, IF it won't "cost" you too much. By cost I mean missed opportunities or puzzled looks from your boss or colleagues who wonder why your profile says something very different from what you are currently doing! By focusing on one job-target, you avoid the risk that your profile will be too scattered, not appealing to any one audience.

For example, I had a client who was a financial controller, but had substantial information technology experience as well. He wanted to move into an I.T. role, so we wrote his resume to focus on his I.T. experience and leadership, and de-emphasize his financial controller background.

But, because he was connected to his boss and a number of other work colleagues on LinkedIn, he could not write the profile the same way as his resume. His boss might have become suspicious when viewing his I.T.-focused profile, since my client was a financial controller! So we had to broaden the profile language beyond the language used in his resume, to encompass both his finance and I.T. experience.

Warning: In case you accidentally open up more than one profile (search under your name if you are unsure), close one down to avoid major confusion in building and updating your network (Note: You cannot transfer connections from one profile to another).

Your Profile has a broader viewing audience
Unlike resumes, it is sometimes not a good idea to list certain specific accomplishments because of the profile's broader viewing audience. You will need to be the judge of when it is or isn't appropriate.

Having a Profile doesn't mean you are looking
While your resume equals "job search," the same is not true for your LinkedIn profile. So should you indicate that you are actively looking for a job or consulting engagement on your profile? The short answer is no.

Now for the long answer. I have known situations where people have been contacted for opportunities with statements in their profile that artfully indicate their search, e.g. "Seeking next exciting challenge" or "Open to select new opportunities." On the other hand, I have talked to recruiters and hiring managers who say that there still is a prejudice against people who are perceived as out of work and actively searching. So a statement indicating you are looking for a job can be divisive—some may be encouraged to contact you, others will be discouraged.

In addition, whether to include these statements goes to the heart of how you approach your search. I advocate an **active** approach to the job search, one where you are going out and getting what you want, not waiting to be found. If you take this approach, indicating that you are looking for a job on your profile becomes less important.

For both of these reasons (that the statements can be viewed negatively and that an active search means being found becomes less of a priority), statements that make it clear you are looking for a job should be left out of a profile.

That said, there are better ways that you can indicate you are open to opportunities without stating it outright and risking turning people off. For example:

- The word "consulting" in your current job title or description indicates, by its very nature, that you are open to other opportunities. Some of you may be in a circumstance to use this word.
- You "may" be able to include in your current position the services you offer employers. For example, you could say something like: "Services include:…" and then list your services in bullet points. Be careful with this if you are not a consultant and are employed full time!

While some may debate these recommendations, here are a couple of rules that are absolutely not debatable:

- Never indicate your openness to opportunities in your 120 character Headline. On LinkedIn, this limited space is valuable real-estate, since it is what people see when they view people-search results. In addition, LinkedIn places a heavy weight on keywords placed in this area when prioritizing profiles to display in search results. Therefore, use this very limited space to pitch an employer with your expertise and brand differentiation-- don't waste it!
- Never put "unemployed" or "looking for a job" on your profile. These phrases have negative connotations and will turn off a potential employer.

The Tone of Profiles vs. Resumes

Because LinkedIn is part of the "social" media universe, it is ok for the profile language to be a little bit more informal than your resume's language. What this means in practice is that you can choose to:

- Use the "Created… Led…" format of the resume where the personal pronouns "I" and "my" are left out
  OR
- Use the slightly more informal personal pronoun format that is generally not accepted in resumes, e.g. "My experience…," or "I led…" That said, always keep your tone professional and appropriate for your job target.

One thing I see on some profiles that you should never do is to adopt the third person, i.e. "Bruce Smith is an accomplished project manager…" That language is too formal even for a resume, and will turn off a number of potential prospects.

Your Profile: the Details

Below are guidelines for filling out select profile sections. "Add Sections" by looking for the sidebar to the right of the LinkedIn edit page, where it will show the sections you can add. Use "keywords" throughout your profile that will help you be found in searches.

1. **Headline:** Fill in this part using up to the 120 characters allowed. Describe how people should categorize you, and if room is left, what makes you different from the competition. For example, if you are targeting Project Management roles in financial services, you might say "Project Manager, Financial Services, with specialty in liaising between IT and business units." Project Manager is the category, and the rest is the differentiation. **Use Keywords!**

2. **Photo:** I recommend adding a business-appropriate one (i.e. it's not a dating service); it adds warmth and personality.

3. **Post an Update:** Skip this, until just before you start inviting people into your network.

4. **Add your positions:** Start with your current or most recent position. Add your education as well. LinkedIn will use the organization names you enter to **suggest people you may know** and want to connect with— helpful in building your network.

   If you are unemployed, consider listing yourself as a consultant (e.g. "Jane Doe Consulting") if you have done anything work-related at all since your last job—even if you were not paid for it. **Volunteering is work experience** (often requiring more skills than your paying gig); you don't need to advertise that you "volunteered," i.e. were paid zero to do this work!

5. **Recommendations:** Skip this for now—they are important, but you are not ready to receive (or give) them yet, since only people you are connected to can give you recommendations.

6. **Summary:** This section is an expanded version of your Headline. Include your "greatest hits" from among your accomplishments, preferably in bullet form (see example profiles mentioned previously).

7. **Skills:** Use the "Skills" section to enter up to 50 keywords, the more the better, as your chances of being "found" will increase.

8. **Personal Information:** I recommend leaving this section blank, since filling it in generally won't make a difference in how effectively you can use LinkedIn for your search.

9. **Contact Settings:** I recommend accepting the defaults (alter as needed).

10. **For Students with Little Work History:** Add additional sections tailored to you, including Projects, Honors & Awards, Courses, Organizations, and Test Scores.

Add Multimedia to Your Profile Sections

When entering profile-edit mode, you'll see the following icons by the Summary section and individual job sections:

Clicking on the middle "add media" icon will enable you to add a presentation, video, image or document. This is an easy way to show off your work. For example, if you are in a creative profession, share some of your creations. Or, share slides from a presentation that demonstrates your expertise.

Just in case you were wondering about the other icons to the left and right of the "add media" icon, the pencil icon to the left enables you to edit each section. The up/down arrow to the right enables you to re-order many of the sections, to, for example, shift the relative positions of the Skills section or individual jobs that you have listed.

How to Be Found

Your profile's content and completeness is key to your being ranked highly in LinkedIn's search results when potential employers are looking.

Be "Relevant"

When people enter keywords to search for potential employees, consultants, presenters, etc. LinkedIn's search results default to a sort "By Relevance." LinkedIn defines relevance by a combination of strength of connections and strength of profile completeness. Specifically, here's how LinkedIn orders searches sorted by Relevance:

1. LinkedIn first sorts by degree of connection. "1st degree connections" are the category of people that show up at the top of a search, then 2nd, then 3rd, then people with which you only share groups. At the bottom of the sort is everyone else.
2. Within each of the sort categories in #1 above, people are then sorted by the degree of profile completeness, with the most complete profiles at the top of each category.

This sort order tells us that 1) having a larger network will increase the likelihood of showing up in searches, and 2) having a complete profile is very important as well to showing up in searches. While this methodology might suggest to you that you should connect with everyone and anyone, this is not necessarily the case. While quantity of connections is clearly important, the quality of connections, should, for most of us, be prioritized before quantity. See the "Strategy for Connecting" subsection that follows under "Building

Your LinkedIn Network" section to learn why.

How to Have a Complete Profile

On the right side of the page, scrolling down a little bit, you should see your "Profile Strength" indicator:

PROFILE STRENGTH

This indicator goes from "Beginner" all the way up to "All Star." You want to get up to the All Star level so that you come up higher in search results. Also, your profile will in general be more impactful if you follow LinkedIn's guidelines for profile strength. You can access these guidelines by clicking on "Improve Your Profile" near the top, just below the photo area:

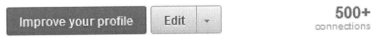

From LinkedIn's blog, LinkedIn considers these items to contribute to maximum profile strength:

- Adding a photo
- Listing "all of your" jobs or positions that you've held *(I take this to mean one or more jobs)*
- Including a description in the jobs or positions that you have listed
- Having five or more skills on your profile
- Filling out the Summary section
- Including your industry
- Adding where you went to school
- Having 50 or more connections

Adding Keywords

Keywords, that is, words that people may use in searches or filters, help your search ranking more in some parts of your profile than others. In particular, keywords in your **Name** (i.e. if they are searching for your name), **Headline, Company Name, Job Title** and **Skills** rank higher in the search results. This is why it is so important to have a 100% complete profile. If these key fields are blank or filled with generic terms, then you fall to the bottom of the search rankings.

Linkedin's various features can help you to identify keywords for both your profile and your resume. I recommend three approaches for researching keywords:

Do an "Advanced Job-postings Search."

Make use of LinkedIn's broad and deep listing of job-postings to identify relevant keywords. Click on "Jobs" in the top menu, then click "Advanced Search," and finally "More Options." You will see a number of search fields that will enable you to fine-tune your search for job postings. Enter keywords that represent job postings in which you may be interested.

For example, if you are looking for a Marketing Director position in the Marketing and Advertising sector, you can enter in the Title field: "Marketing AND Director AND NOT (analysis OR analytics)." Note, the connectors (AND, OR, NOT) must be capitalized. Then, select the appropriate industry. The result: you will find job postings for the industry you selected that have these keywords in the posting title.

Once you have found two or three postings that match your job target, review them to look for keywords. For example, when I performed this exact search, I found additional keywords like "digital marketing," "cross-channel marketing," "communications," and "campaigns."

Create a "Word Cloud" for the Job Postings you found

Word clouds enable you to visually see the frequency of words that show up in a block of text. If you google "Word Cloud" you will see the many free tools that can enable you to create word clouds. I use "TagCrowd" at www.tagcrowd.com.

Copy the job description text from each of the two or three postings that you found into one "word cloud." I copied the text from the combined job descriptions into the WordCrowd input box, checking off "100 words maximum" and "show frequency." I then clicked "visualize" and additional keywords jumped out, including "leadership," "management," and "clients."

Do an "Advanced People Search."

Select "people" from the dropdown menu to the left of the search box on top of the LinkedIn page. Then click on the "advanced" link that appears to the right of the search box.

Enter the same search criteria that you used for Title and Industry in the "Advanced Job-postings Search," with one addition: make sure you select "current" after you enter keywords in the Title field, so that these keywords are in the user's current job title. Browse through the LinkedIn profiles of those people that you found through this search, with a specific focus on the "skills" section of their profile, to identify keywords.

By the way, I discuss the <u>Advanced People Search</u> feature in more detail in the *Using LinkedIn* section later in this chapter.

Test Your Profile's "Searchability"

Incorporate the most relevant keywords that you have come up with in the most important sections for keywords (Name, Headline, Company Name, Job Title and Skills). Now search LinkedIn for those keywords. For example, if you think people will look for you by entering "Graphic Designer" then type these words in quotes (so LinkedIn sees it as a phrase) in the People Search box, as shown below.

If you don't show up on the first page of results, update these sections to include those relevant terms and then search again. For example, if your current job title says "Consultant," change it to "Graphic Design Consultant." You'll actually see yourself moving up the ranks each time you improve the number and placement of your keywords.

Getting Recommendations

You can get recommendations from people in your 1st degree network by sending out a recommendation request. These recommendations enhance your marketability. Simply select "Profile," then "Recommendations" from the dropdown menu, then select "Request Recommendations" on the new window that opens up. Then choose the person from whom you want the recommendation in your 1st degree network.

When you request the recommendation, include in your request the areas of your experience that you want emphasized. This will make it easier for the person to write the recommendation, and you are more likely to get a high-quality one. Once a person writes a recommendation, you will be notified by email. You can then choose whether to accept it, ask for a revision, ignore or decline it.

Do not accept weak recommendations, as they can potentially hurt you. For example, one of my clients received a recommendation that read: "I worked with Mary for two years. Mary was in charge of budgeting for our division.

Mary is very detail oriented." The content is factual, but does not indicate how well Mary did her job, leaving this question hanging uncomfortably. Much stronger would be: "Mary did a great job ensuring that the budget was completed accurately, and on schedule."

People may also ask you for a recommendation. If you feel positive about the person, I would encourage you to write it. Beyond it being just a nice, generous thing to do, this gesture will appear in your network's weekly digest (see next section), and thus increase your visibility.

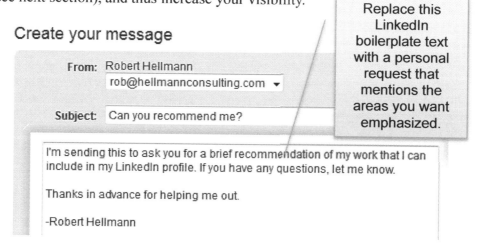

Endorsements vs. Recommendations

LinkedIn has added a controversial "Endorsements" feature. I say it is controversial because many people (including myself) feel it is just too easy to click on the endorsement button. The result is too many endorsements for things that you actually did not do for those who endorsed you, which reduces the effectiveness of this whole feature. I've spoken to recruiters and they consistently disparage this feature, discounting it in their decision-making process, for this reason. On the other hand, LinkedIn Recommendations are valued by recruiters both because of the effort involved and the more descriptive nature of the recommendations.

So, should you bother to get endorsements? The answer is both No and Yes. Don't go out of your way, for the reasons I describe above. BUT, if you have a lot of endorsements, it does look like you have at least something going for you. That is, a high volume of endorsements says at least that you are good at getting endorsements! Plus it suggests that all these people who have endorsed you like (or don't dislike) you. In that sense, a large volume of endorsements can add something positive to your profile.

Personally, I wish LinkedIn never added the Endorsements feature. Recommendations are more than enough. But since the feature is there, if you are very motivated, then it will only help if you have a lot of endorsements.

Here's a screenshot of my Skills section, with accompanying endorsements, as of October 14th, 2013. By the time you read this, perhaps LinkedIn will have improved this feature and made it more effective.

Building Your LinkedIn Network

Now that you have a decent profile, you can start to build your network and your visibility. One of LinkedIn's primary values is in its ability to both keep you "connected" with your **1st degree network**, and get introduced to your **2nd and 3rd degree extended network**.

Strategy for Connecting

For most professions and job searches, the best strategy for developing your

LinkedIn network is **quality first, then quantity** (with some exceptions discussed in the next section). Quality means:

a) You know them in some way (even if only barely) and you might be open to helping them/they might be open to helping you. This category includes, for example, someone you had a good 20 minute conversation with at a conference and want to keep in touch with, b) someone you worked with 10 years ago, haven't talked to since, and they didn't dislike you, c) family, friends, your dentist, etc.

b) You don't know them, but they reach out to you first and after looking at their profile, you want them in your network. You will want to selectively accept requests to connect from people you don't know, if their background, connections or character make them someone who you would welcome in your network. The reason: because they initiated the request to connect, they are self-selecting for being more open to facilitating an introduction on your behalf.

Since I like to know everyone in my network, i.e. have a quality network based on real relationships, here's what I do when I get a request from someone I don't know. I reply by email to the connection request I receive in my email inbox, and say: *"Thank you for reaching out. As I like to know everyone in my first degree network, what prompted you to reach out to me and/or how did you come across my profile?"* If they never bother to respond to this email, I don't bother accepting their connection request. On the other hand, I've built some nice new professional relationships by reaching out this way!

One client already had 1,000-plus connections when we began working together. When he tried using LinkedIn to find people to whom he could reach out, he found the experience frustrating because the quality of his network was poor—reaching out to these strangers for introductions was not productive. In addition, his weekly email digest containing his network's activity on LinkedIn was meaningless to him. Ultimately, he removed many connections (by clicking on "Contacts" under the "Network" option, selecting the contacts he wanted to remove, then selecting "Remove from Contacts" under the "More" dropdown) and LinkedIn began to be more useful to him.

The bottom line: make the connection if you could see a possibility of either 1) being open to facilitating an introduction on behalf of this person, or 2) reaching out to them for an introduction.

Note: if you invite people to connect who are complete strangers: They can respond by clicking on "I don't know this user." After several of these messages, LinkedIn automatically restricts your use!

The Exception to this Strategy

If you are a recruiter either internally or for an agency, meaning your career success depends on finding the right people for positions, you may want to re-prioritize your strategy to favor quantity over quality. The reason: LinkedIn's usefulness to you may be greater as a database of potential job prospects than it will be as a pure networking tool. By connecting with the whole world, you are improving your ability to search for and find people, and communicate open positions. This benefit comes from LinkedIn enabling you to a) view the profiles of everyone in your first degree network, b) directly message up to 50 of them at a time to alert them about positions, and c) advertise positions via your "Status Update."

Another possible exception where you would choose quantity first before quality is if you solely want to use LinkedIn passively, to be found by other people in their searches. Then, of course, the more 1st degree connections you have, the more likely you'll come up in searches.

BUT, I do not advocate this passive strategy for using LinkedIn. My whole approach, the one that works best for clients, is an **active** one. That is, you don't want to be out there in the ocean, just drifting with the currents hoping they'll take you to the island of your dreams. You want to actively find the island you want to swim to, and then swim to it! LinkedIn is just a wonderful tool for this active approach, For most of us not in the business of finding people to fill positions, putting quality first, then quantity, improves LinkedIn's effectiveness for this kind of active career management.

Inviting Others to Connect

First select "Contacts" from the top menu, then "Add Connections." You will then be presented with options for how to add contacts (pictured below). The fastest option for building your network quickly is by importing your address book into LinkedIn.

See Who You Already Know on LinkedIn

M	@	O	Y!		Aol.	
Gmail	Your Email	Outlook	Yahoo! Mail	Hotmail	AOL	Any Email

Get started by adding your email address.

Your email

rob@hellmannconsulting.com

Continue   🔒 **Your contacts are safe with us!**
We'll import your address book to suggest connections and help you manage your contacts. And we won't store your password or email anyone without your permission. Learn More

An alternate, slower way to build your network is by sending invitations one at a time. When you send invitations, ideally you would want to personalize the invite, beyond just the standard boilerplate text that LinkedIn gives you. In particular, if the person might not remember you, remind her/him how you know each other. You can quickly find people to send invitations to individually in two ways:

1. On the top right of your Profile page, you will see "People You May Know." Click on the link, and you will see pages of suggestions for people you may know. LinkedIn provides these suggestions based on the organizations and schools (and the associated time-frames) that you have listed on your profile. Having a complete list of organizations with the right spelling will help LinkedIn suggest people you may know to you.

2. Search the name of someone you want to connect with in the "People" search window on the upper right of any page.

Then select his or her name and the profile will come up. You can then scroll to the right and click on "Connect."

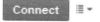

Accepting Requests to Connect

When someone sends a request to you to connect, you will receive a LinkedIn notification in your email about it. You will also see the connection request in your Inbox on LinkedIn. If you click on the "Invitation to Connect" link, you will see the invitation, including these options:

If you get a request from someone you either don't know or don't want to connect with, I recommend that you ignore the request to connect by clicking "Ignore" or literally just ignore it.

Once you click "Ignore" you will be presented with another option: "I don't know this user." Keep in mind that clicking it **may cause problems for the person sending the invite**; too many of these responses will result in his or her account being automatically restricted. Also, you will be prevented from receiving future invites from this account.

Join LinkedIn Groups

LinkedIn groups help you connect with people you may not know to build new professional relationships and learn from group discussions. You can search for people in your groups who work in companies or at jobs in which you are interested, and then message them through LinkedIn.

Which Groups to Join
Join groups that have at least one of the following features:
- ✓ A large number of employed members, ideally at organizations that comprise your job target.
- ✓ Active, thoughtful discussions about topics relating to your job target.
- ✓ Members who theoretically could be in a position to hire you.

Although some groups are well moderated and prevent people from posting annoying personal sales pitches, others may have no moderation at all. Many of these groups do not feature meaningful discussions. Still, even these un-moderated groups can be valuable if the members work in the places that interest you, because **you can message them via LinkedIn**.

To get started, look at associations you already belong to, such as your alumni or professional association, as they may have LinkedIn groups. You can search for groups by selecting "Groups" in the dropdown to the left of the search box (red arrow), and then entering a topic. Or, select "Groups" from the top menu under "Interests."

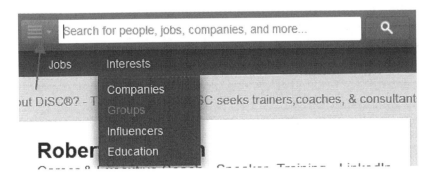

Say one of your targets is Project Management. Select Groups from the dropdown menu by the search box, then enter "Project Management." You'll see many relevant groups appear, some that have active discussions. An alternative is to click on "Groups" on the main menu, then select "Find a Group" by scrolling to the right. You can then search by keyword and group category.

Most groups have a little "lock" icon next to their name, indicating that you need to be approved to get in the group. Often this simply means having the right keywords in your Profile. For example, someone joining the Binghamton Alumni group would need to have Binghamton listed in the Education section. Sometimes, though, the approval process is more involved.

One quick way to see if a group has high quality discussions that you might learn from or contribute to is to click on "Group Statistics" by scrolling down a bit and looking for this icon on the right. Once you've clicked on this icon, you will see a list of menu options. Click on "Activity" as pictured below.

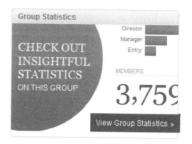

You will then see two numbers, representing "Discussions" (the number of posts on a new topic) and "Comments" (the number of comments on each new topic). You will also see a graph of how these numbers have changed over time. The best groups have a relatively high ratio of Comments to Discussions (usually that means a ratio of "1" or higher), which indicates that the discussion topics that people post are generating a good amount of commentary!

The picture that follows shows a group I belong to (*the Organization Development Network*) that has very interesting, useful, thoughtful discussions targeted to professionals in the field. You can see that the ratio of Comments to Discussions is high (at 230/41, way above 1). Too often though, the numbers are reversed, indicating that people in this group are not paying attention to the discussion topics, or that the topics themselves are of poor quality (e.g. "Buy my Seven Steps to Success…").

COMMENTS LAST WEEK

DISCUSSIONS LAST WEEK

COMMENTS AND DISCUSSIONS

230

41

PROMOTIONS LAST WEEK

300
200
100
0

When you click on a group that you have joined, you will see new menu options, as pictured for one of my groups.

Two options that can help you to identify opportunities for building new relationships include 1) "Discussions" and 2) the Members Directory, accessed by clicking on "Members." Other noteworthy menu options include "Jobs" (for jobs that are posted by group members—these are different from LinkedIn "Jobs").

Notating & "Tagging" Your Network

LinkedIn has features that help you to remember how you know a 1st degree contact, as well as categorize contacts by "tags" that you define. Since my networking strategy is to maintain a "quality" network, I regularly notate and tag contacts to remember how I know them, and to segment them into pre-defined groups (i.e. tag them) for possible outreach.

These two features are explained in more detail below:

To Save Notes on a 1st degree Contact's Profile
Click on "Note" near the top of your 1st degree connection's profile, just below their picture (see clip that follows):

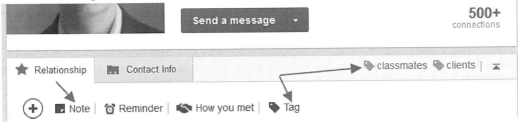

To "Tag" Your 1st Degree Contacts
This feature can be useful not only to help you remember how you know someone, but also to send out a targeted message to a particular category of connections, if you have a question you want to ask them (e.g. "Does anyone know a person with…" or "What are the best blogs in…", etc.). In the screenshot above, I assigned two "tags" to this 1st degree contact: "classmates" and "clients." You can customize and tags – you don't need

to use the default list.

You can also assign tags to a number of contacts at once.
1) Click on the "Contacts" menu option under "Network" as shown below.
2) Search for contacts.
3) Check the box to the left of the contacts that you want to tag.
4) Click on the "tags" link (red arrow). You'll then see a list of tags. You can add/delete tags, and check off one or more tags that apply to the contacts you've selected.

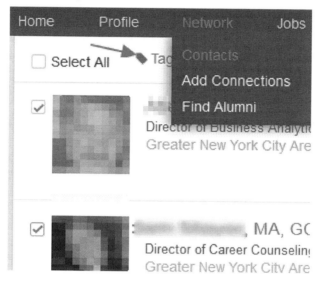

Using LinkedIn

Now that you've created your profile, begun building your network, and joined groups, you are ready to start using LinkedIn's powerful career advancement and job-search features. We will cover the following capabilities:
- ✓ Career research
- ✓ Finding people in companies or industries
- ✓ How to contact the people you find
- ✓ Answering LinkedIn ads
- ✓ Keeping in touch with your network
- ✓ Additional thoughts for consultants or business owners
- ✓ LinkedIn's utility on-the-job

Career Research
For this section, we'll explore ways that LinkedIn can help you with:

- Researching Career Options
- Developing Your Target List of Companies
- Viewing Profiles for Pre-Meeting Preparation
- Posing Questions to Your Network

Researching Career Options:

Let's take a look at three ways you can research career options: LinkedIn "Alumni," "Jobs," and "Today."

LinkedIn "Alumni"

I work with a number of clients who are considering going back to school or are deciding what to focus on while in school. LinkedIn's "Alumni" feature has been helpful to them in understanding how different educational choices correlate with careers. Here's how to use this feature:

1) Go to www.linkedin.com/alumni
2) Choose a college or university by selecting from the menu or search option on the right. In the picture below, "Fordham Graduate School of Business" was automatically selected for me because it's one of the schools I attended, as per my profile.
3) You will see columns that divide alumni by where they work, what they do, and so forth. Scroll to the right until you see "What they studied" and "What they're skilled at."
4) In the example below, I selected to view the 82 profiles of people who studied "English Language and Literature" and graduated from Fordham's graduate business school. Note that LinkedIn includes in this group people who studied this subject at any school listed on their profile- that is, they may not have studied this subject at Fordham.
5) Now, you can look at the profiles of these people to learn more about their career trajectory.

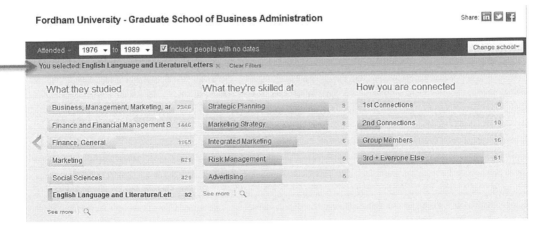

LinkedIn "Jobs"

Click on "Jobs" in the top menu, then select "Advanced Search," and finally "more options." You will find a highly customizable search feature for job postings. Looking at job postings is a great way to explore career options. For example:

- Type in a skill in the "keywords" section. For example, you can enter the entire phrase:

  "financial planning" OR "financial analysis"

  Yes LinkedIn lets you enter Boolean search strings such as AND, OR, NOT, (), and also use quotes to search on phrases.
- Select one or more industries from the industry list.
- Enter keywords or phrases in the "Job Title" window—which also allows Boolean search strings.

Not only will you find lists of job postings where you can see what skills and keywords are incorporated, but also people in your network who work at the companies listed, and sometimes the person who posted the position! Consider reaching out to one or more of these people for an informational meeting, to further your job target research (or perhaps apply for the job!).

LinkedIn "Today"

This feature allows you to receive custom news feeds right to your email inbox on topics that interest you. I (and clients) have found it to be very useful in keeping up to date with what's going on within a specific industry or profession.

Go to www.linkedin.com/today and click the "Setup" icon to the right. You can customize the type of news you receive in your inbox, by industry/profession.

Develop Your Target List of Companies

One of the foundations of a productive job search involves developing a plan to market yourself, including a list of the companies that you want to pursue by job target. This way you are being proactive in getting what you want, and not just waiting for the ad to show up or the headhunter to call. LinkedIn is ideal for setting up this list of companies. To develop your company list, use a combination of:

- company searches
- company "Insights" from within a company page
- advanced people searches
- alumni searches

Let's look at how you would go about using each of these features.

Company Searches

A client was interested in moving into the Private Equity sector. He wanted to create a list of companies to which he could proactively reach out, but didn't know where to start. So here's what we did:

1) From the top menu, we clicked on *"Companies"* (under "Interests"), then *"Search Companies"* at the top for an advanced search. The result: we saw advanced search options in the left column of the page.
2) We typed "New York" in the *enter location name* text box, and then selected from the resulting options "Greater New York City Area."
3) Under *Industry* we typed "Private Equity" and then selected from the resulting options "Venture Capital & Private Equity."
4) The result was a list of Private Equity firms in the greater New York City area. Since my client was interested in the largest firms, we then selected *"Company Size"* and chose the largest firms. Not only did this list give my client the companies for his marketing plan, it also suggested people in his network that he could reach out to for each company.

Company "Insights"

Another client used the Company Search feature in a different way. She was interested in the Pharmaceutical industry, in particular Pfizer and its competitors. But she didn't know who its competitors were. Here's what she did:

1) From the top menu, she clicked on "Companies" then "Search Companies."
2) She then entered "Pfizer" in the text box, and selected the company from the resulting options.
3) She was now on Pfizer's "Company Page." From the Company Page menu, she selected "Insights."
4) On the "Insights" page, she found what she was looking for in two places. First, she noticed on the top left a section entitled "Where Employees Came From." This list gave her some ideas for Pfizer competitors that she could approach.

WHERE EMPLOYEES CAME FROM

Merck (824)
GlaxoSmithKline (751)
Bristol-Myers Squibb (451)
Sanofi (436)
Novartis (404)

Second, she saw at the bottom a section called "People Also Viewed."
Many pharmaceutical company competitors were listed here as well.

PEOPLE ALSO VIEWED

Novartis
Pharmaceuticals

GlaxoSmithKline
Pharmaceuticals

Johnson & Johnson
Hospital and Health
Care

Merck
Pharmaceuticals

Sanofi
Pharmaceuticals

AstraZeneca
Pharmaceuticals

Both of these sections gave her a list of companies that were related to Pfizer,
which she could consider for her marketing plan.

Advanced People Searches – by Region

Advanced People Searches are great for finding specific people to reach out
to. Using it for this purpose will be covered in detail in a later section. In this
section, however, I want to highlight how it can be used to find companies in
a new geographic area.

For example, I had a client who was a "PeopleSoft" programmer (this is a
software package that is used by many HR departments). He was
contemplating a move from New York to Philadelphia, but didn't know which
companies (if any) in the area might hire people with his skill. Here's what
we did to find out.

1) By the search box on the top of the page, we made sure "People" was
selected by clicking on the dropdown to the left of the search box, and
then clicked on "Advanced" to the right.

2) For the "Title" text box, we entered "PeopleSoft" and selected "Current" just below the text box, so that our search would turn up people with "PeopleSoft" in their current job title.
3) For the "Location" menu option, we selected "Located In or Near" and then entered one of the zip codes in Philadelphia, that we found by clicking on the adjacent "Lookup" link. We then selected "Within 50 miles."
4) After pressing "Search" we found a list of people with "PeopleSoft" in their job titles, and the names of the companies at which they worked. Companies included Canon, Toll Brothers, ADP, Vanguard, Conde Nast, and many more.

My client now had a company list that he could begin to use for his outreach, as well as a list of people at those companies whom he could potentially contact.

Advanced People Search to See Where Former Colleagues Went

Do an Advanced People Search, but instead of selecting "current" under the "Company" keyword search box, select "Past Not Current." You can then see where people went who used to work at your company (Pfizer in the example below).

You can then refine these search results further in the left column that appears next to your results, e.g. add a "current" Title or Keywords to select for people who are in your field. Not only do you get more information about possible companies to target, but you now have a nice lead-in for an introductory message, e.g. *"I see you used to work at Pfizer as a Finance Director. I'm still there, am a Finance Director myself, and am wondering how things compare..."*

View Profiles for pre-Meeting Research
This ability to view profiles of people you may be meeting in an interview situation, or may want to meet, is a fundamental value that LinkedIn provides.

For example, at one time I wanted to transition my career from the financial services sector to higher education. One person I wanted to meet, the number two person at an Ivy League school, had a LinkedIn profile that showed he himself had transitioned from financial services to higher education many years prior. I used this knowledge as a way of approaching him, relating his situation earlier in life to my current one. For this reason and a variety of others, I was able to get the meeting with him that I sought.

Pose Questions to Your Network
You can send a message via LinkedIn to anyone in your first degree network. Consider taking advantage of the "tags" feature to send out a targeted message to your network. For example, you might ask questions…

- …pertaining to expertise in a particular profession or industry. A client asked a segment of her network about the best blogs and resources for the advertising industry.
- …about hiring needs for your firm or department, e.g. "Can anyone recommend a top-notch programmer…"

Find People in Companies/Industries
LinkedIn is a fantastic tool for finding the "right" people to whom you want to reach out. We'll cover several methods in detail for finding contact opportunities:
- ✓ LinkedIn Companies
- ✓ LinkedIn Alumni
- ✓ LinkedIn Groups
- ✓ Advanced People Search
- ✓ Searching a 1st Degree Connection's contacts

Finding Contacts via LinkedIn "Companies"
Use this feature as another way to see with whom you are connected in your target companies, to ensure that you didn't miss any potential contact opportunities. Select "*Interests*" from the top menu, then "*Companies*" from the dropdown menu. Then enter the name of the company in which you are interested. For example, when I type "Pfizer," it gives me:
- A high-level summary of the company.
- Everyone in my extended network who works, or has worked, there.
- Recent news about new hires.
- Company offices and locations.
- The top companies that people who work for Pfizer leave for, or came from— giving you additional companies to target in your search.
- Job openings posted through LinkedIn.

You can follow a company and receive notifications of company profile changes, new hires, job postings, and so forth. In the company search box, specify industry or other criteria to develop a target list of companies.

Finding Contacts Using the "Alumni" Feature

Alumni are potentially a great source for informational meetings that could lead to interviews. LinkedIn has a feature that simplifies the process of figuring out to which of your alumni you want to reach out. Go to www.linkedin.com/alumni.

You will then see a screen that lists your alumni and how you are connected to them, for one of the schools listed in your profile. Even more useful, your alumni are categorized by company, profession and region. Click on one of the categories for a targeted list of alumni. You will also see an option to change the school, to view schools that you didn't even attend!

Where they work...		What they do...		Where they live...	
IBM	61	Entrepreneur	728	United States	3617
Citi	18	Information technology	202	Greater New York City Area	1606
Binghamton University	17	Finance	193	Greater Boston Area	179
JPMorgan Chase	14	Engineering	188	Washington D.C. Metro Area	175
Pfizer	13	Administrative	106	Ithaca, New York Area	160
show more...		show more...		show more...	

Also see the LinkedIn Alumni section under Researching Career Options to learn about additional value that this feature provides.

Group Discussions

Use groups (see "Join LinkedIn Groups" under "Getting Set Up") to learn how you can help potential employers, and to interact with people with whom you may want to connect. You can gain valuable insight from the postings of professionals in your field.

In addition, LinkedIn groups have a feature that allows you to click on "Follow This Discussion" or "Follow John Doe," so when a new post is added to the discussion, or when John posts something new, you will be alerted via email. This feature makes it easier to keep track of group discussions and people that you want to contact or learn from.

For those groups where there are active, thoughtful discussions, you may want to be notified daily by email regarding new discussion activity. You can set your preferences for group email notifications by clicking on "*Settings*," then "*Groups, Companies and Applications*" on the left, and finally "*Set the frequency of group digest notifications."*

Use "Advanced People Search" for Organizations and Industries

Now that you have started to build up your network and you have joined groups, you can use LinkedIn's powerful "advanced people search" feature to find people to contact. Once you identify the appropriate people, either contact them directly or get introduced through your network.

To demonstrate, I'll share an example of a client, Sarah, who was interested in a marketing manager or director position at Pfizer, in or near New York City. Here's what my client did:

1. She clicked on "Advanced," to the right of the "people" search box on the upper right, to get a screen full of options to narrow down her search.

2. Under "Location," she selected "In or Near" her zip code, then "within 50 miles."

3. Under "Relationship" she checked "All LinkedIn Members."

4. She kept "Sort by Relevance" (experiment with these sort options to vary the results).

5. Under "Company," she entered "Pfizer," then from the dropdown menu she selected "Current," meaning the results will show only people who currently work there. Note: Sarah could also have used the "Industries" menu option, instead of "Company," and selected Pharmaceuticals, if she wanted a broader industry search.

6. She then clicked on "Search" at the bottom.

(Note: Search options will include greyed out items with a 🔲 symbol next to them, meaning these options are available for a fee. In most cases you won't need these options.)

Her result: Thousands of entries came up. Within the first couple of pages she saw many 2nd degree connections (people who her 1st degree contacts could introduce her to) working at Pfizer. But she realized she was not getting enough senior marketing people in her results-- that is, people in a position to hire her. So she refined her search by adding the following criteria:

> For "Title" she entered: **Marketing AND (Senior OR VP OR SVP OR Executive OR Chief OR "Vice President") AND NOT "Senior Manager"** . She also selected "current" to indicate that these keywords had to be in their current job title.

This character string employs *Boolean Logic* such as "AND" , "OR" (these need to be capitalized) and parentheses to get her the more senior level marketing professionals that she was looking for. She also used quotations so that LinkedIn would search for the entire phrase "Vice President" rather than "Vice" OR "President."

The result: my client found the potential hiring managers at Pfizer that she was looking for, including a Senior Vice President- Marketing, Senior Director/Group Leader- Consumer Marketing, and a VP - Head of Global Marketing & Brand Strategy. The first two of these were second degree connections, and she shared a group with the third one. She could reach out to this "group only" contact by messaging him directly through LinkedIn.

Try Selecting "Group" instead of "All LinkedIn Members"
The default in "Advanced People Search" is to show results that include all LinkedIn Members. If you select "Group" instead, results will be shown for only those members that share one or more groups with you. The advantage of trying this is that you will get different results, and the results may be better-- the people on top will often have more connection points with you.

For example, when I just did an Advanced People Search using the default "All..." criteria, the top-ranked result registered two shared connections. When I then did the same search but changed the criteria to "Groups" the top-ranked result registered two shared connections plus two shared groups! The person represented by this latter result is easier to contact, because a) I can message them directly through the group, and b) the message may resonate more because we have more connection points that I can refer to in my note (four vs. two).

If a Search Result lists only the Last Name's initial
If the person is a third degree or group-only contact, then you will usually only see the first initial of the last name. To find the full name, try typing in Google, for example, "LinkedIn Robert" plus the title and company (or other profile information) just as it is written in the LinkedIn search listing. Most of the time you will see the full name and LinkedIn profile in Google's search results. If the contact is from a shared group, you can also try entering the information you do have in a group-members-search; the result should show you the full name.

Searching a First Degree Connection's Contacts (or your own contacts)
Sometimes people in your LinkedIn network, with large networks of their

own, will generously offer their contacts up for you to browse and request and introduction. When a 1st degree connection has a large amount of their own contacts, however, you'll need to use LinkedIn's contact search capability to preempt having to painstakingly browse through endless pages of your connection's contacts. Here's how it works:

1) Go to your contact's profile page.
2) Scroll down until you're almost at the bottom. You will see a section called "Connections" (unless your contact's settings prevent you from seeing them).
3) On the top right of this section, you'll see a magnifying glass. Click on it.

4) Type a search string. It almost doesn't matter what you type here, because the key is to get the results—where you'll be able to see a link for "Advanced Search" and get a slew of additional search options.
5) Once you click on Advanced Search, you'll see a sidebar on the left with many options that will help you to narrow down your search. For example, you will see "keywords," industry," "school," and so forth.

By the way, you can use this same feature to easily search your own contacts. Just follow these same steps for your own profile.

How to Contact People that You Find

Practically speaking, there are five channels to contact people you meet on LinkedIn. These are:

- ❖ Email
- ❖ Groups
- ❖ InMail
- ❖ Introductions
- ❖ Request to Connect

Let's talk about each of these channels. Note that I'm leaving out letter writing, which for most intents and purposes is not practical given then prevalence and ease of email. See my Appendix discussion on the topic for more about the pros and cons.

Email vs. Messaging through LinkedIn

LinkedIn is a wonderful tool for finding the right people to contact. Just because you've found the right people via LinkedIn, however, it doesn't mean that you have to message them through LinkedIn. In fact, in many cases you may prefer to try and email them! Everyone is comfortable with email, and is accustomed to getting messages from all sorts of people through this channel. Comfort with messages via LinkedIn is less consistent, which may result in a lower response rate. Judge each situation on a case-by-case basis in terms of choosing messaging via LinkedIn vs. email. I've included the example in the box that follows to illustrate further how to write these messages.

Messaging via a Group

If you can't find their email address, perhaps you share a group with them. If so, in most cases you can message people right through the group. Here's what you do:

1) Go to the group.
2) Click on "Members" (see red arrow in picture that follows)

3) Enter their name in the search box.
4) You will see "Send Message" as one of the options by the people that show up.

What follows is an example of a message that a client sent to a fellow group member. Note, that she could have easily sent this same message via email as well. This message resulted in an informational meeting which led to two referrals, and ultimately an interview (that's how it works—one thing leads to another and then another until finally you get the result you want).

A client sent a LinkedIn message to someone she didn't know. This message resulted in a meeting and referral for an interview.

| 1. Focus on value to them |
| 2. Asked for just 20 minutes |
| 3. Mutually beneficial |
| 4. Powerful Pitch |
| 5. Not asking for a job |
| 6. No reference to a resume |
| 7. Call to action |

Dear Claire,

Upon seeing your name in the AFP LinkedIn Group and noticing our additional shared connection, I thought I would reach out to you; I myself have many years of experience with fundraising.

I'm currently a Director of Alumni and Event Planning at Ivy University. In the long run I am looking to transition outside of higher-ed, to a non-profit such as GoodOrg. Though not yet looking for a job, I would greatly appreciate 20 minutes of your time to gain your insight on how my experience might fit in a non-profit setting. Given my many years of experience developing successful fundraising strategies and events, perhaps I could also share with you some ideas that you would find useful for GoodOrg's efforts.

Some background: As you can see from my profile, I have over 10 years of experience in fundraising and event planning that could be useful to non-profits. Highlights include:

- Developed an approach, working with IT, to identify most likely donors, which resulted in a 37% increase in donations following its implementation.
- Led a capital campaign last year that brought in $3 million and exceeded goals.
- Created partnerships with associations that provided new value to alumni; these partnerships were credited with substantially increasing donations.
- Planned and delivered a new alumni event that exceeded fundraising forecasts, and was so successful that it has been instituted indefinitely on an annual basis.

I would greatly value your insight regarding this hoped-for transition. Would you be available for a brief conversation, either in person or by phone?

How to Ask for an Introduction

One of LinkedIn's killer applications is its ability to leverage your "first degree network" to get introductions to your second or third degree contacts. My clients make use of these introductions (as do I) for various reasons, including a job search, new business/career opportunities, as a recruiting tool, or just to learn from others. Here's how to write an introduction request that will get you the meeting you want.

The Six Things to Include in Your Introduction Request

The bottom line: make it easy for your first degree connection to forward your meeting request. Let's take an example based on a client's situation. Ellen wanted to meet Susan, a second degree connection, and she saw that John was their mutual first degree connection. Ellen's introduction request to John contained these six elements, in the sequence below:

1) Start with the reason for your message: Ellen began with *"Hi John, I see that Susan Smith is in your first-degree network. I would very much appreciate an introduction to her for a 10 minute conversation."* Note—asking for just 10 minutes makes it very easy for John to forward that connection, since everyone has 10 minutes available somewhere on their calendar. Also, note the word "appreciate." I'm amazed at how many clients forget to show appreciation or gratitude when asking for something!

2) Then say why you want the meeting: *"I noticed that Susan works in alumni relations at Ivy University. Over the long term, I'm very interested in making a move into higher education. I would welcome the opportunity to get Susan's perspective on how the school is organized and where I might be able to add value down the road."*

3) Say you won't ask for a job: Ellen took the pressure off by specifically saying she won't be asking for a job. *"In the conversation I seek, I will not be asking Susan about job openings; Rather, I'm looking to gain her insight into Ivy and possibly other institutions of higher-ed."*

4) Make the request mutually beneficial: Your first degree connection is much more likely to pass on your request if she/he feels they are helping both you and the other person in their first degree network (and your intended recipient is much more likely to respond positively). *"I believe this meeting will be mutually beneficial. Given my many years of experience in fundraising, I could share with Susan some ideas that she may find useful for her efforts."*

5) Include your "pitch" about how you can help an organization: You'll generate more enthusiasm for the meeting by doing this. Ellen wrote: *"Susan may be interested to know that I have 10 years of experience in fundraising at non-profits, as is shown on my LinkedIn profile. During that time, I:*
   - *Met or exceeded every annual fundraising goal for the past 10 years*
   - *Planned and delivered dozens of successful events*
   - *etc. ...*

6) Give your 1st degree an out. Perhaps John has sent too many introduction requests to Susan, or he is uncomfortable passing on this request for other reasons. Ellen still wants to maintain a good, respectful relationship with John! *"If you feel that it is not appropriate to pass on this request, I totally understand. Regardless, I hope we stay in touch. Let me know if there's anything I can do for you."*

Where to Click in LinkedIn to Request an Introduction
In the example that follows, I've identified a 2nd degree contact, To get

introduced through my first degree connection, I would scroll to the right, click the drop-down arrow next to "Connect" and select "Get Introduced."

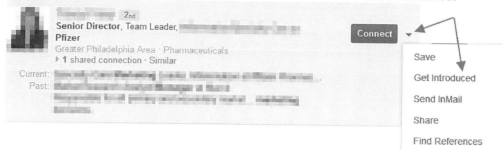

I then select my first degree connection who can make the introduction, and click "send message."

Consider Sending the Introduction Request via Email
Just because you found the connection on LinkedIn, it doesn't mean that you need to send your introduction request via LinkedIn as well. In fact, email is often the preferred channel. The reason: we're all too familiar with our email inbox, but many people show lesser levels of comfort and responsiveness with LinkedIn messages. I've seen cases where individuals are unresponsive to LinkedIn messages, but respond immediately to an email (the reverse seems to be less true).

Therefore, I recommend that you default to using email to send your introduction request. Use LinkedIn to request the introduction only if a) you don't have your first degree connection's email address, or b) your first degree connection prefers that you request the introduction via LinkedIn. Whether you use email or LinkedIn to request your introduction, the key points you need to include are the same.

Other Thoughts
You might say to yourself "why bother with this message if I'm not asking for a job?" The reason is that these types of meetings give you access to the "hidden job market." By meeting with a number of the "right" people this way, and keeping in touch, you absolutely will begin to get referrals for interviews, or they'll think of you first when something opens up. See this post and this one (and this one) for more on the hidden job market.

Consider Contacting the Person Directly: Maybe you barely know the person in your network who can introduce you. Or, perhaps you have less than stellar confidence in how your first degree connection might represent you in an introduction. Or maybe time is of the essence— and this type of networking can take time! In these cases, you may want to send an email (or LinkedIn Group message) directly to the person you are seeking to meet, saying in the subject line "<u>Our mutual shared connections on LinkedIn</u>" or something similar.

Fully Leverage LinkedIn's Ability to Find the Right People: Use diverse LinkedIn tools including "Advanced People Searches," "Company Pages," your Groups, and LinkedIn's Alumni tool, to find people to connect with.

Making an introduction can benefit you as well. When you introduce Bob to Anne, you create an opportunity to send a networking message to Anne as part of the introduction. You can say: "and by the way, I've heard about all the things going on in your company. We should grab coffee sometime and catch up!"

If Someone Asks You for an Introduction

When someone asks you for an introduction, ask the requestor to write why it would be in their mutual interest to connect with your contact. This way, when making the introduction, you can feel confident that you are adding value for both parties in your network.

Using InMail

LinkedIn's "InMail" feature allows you to send anyone on LinkedIn a message, for a price. The fee is currently $5 per InMail, with a limit of 5 per month. If you buy a premium membership, a select number of InMails are included. So, do they work? Sometimes, but in my opinion not enough to place them above these other "free" methods. The drawback to InMail is that many people don't seem to read or respond well to them. My informal research says that this is because 1) many people are only nominally on LinkedIn, and may just ignore or delete messages from LinkedIn, and 2) InMail is usually used when there is no other way to connect with the person. Being that it's from a complete stranger and there is a fee element to it, many view InMails as spam.

That said, some people do have success with InMails. Plus, LinkedIn offers your money back if you pay for an InMail and you don't get a response. So, try it, but only if the other methods discussed here (emails, group messages, introduction requests) are not working for a particular person you want to contact.

Sending a "Request to Connect" Message

When you find someone's profile and click the "Connect" button, you are of course able to send a brief message. The problem with this approach in most cases, however, is the character limit of 300 for the message. This simply does not provide the space necessary to convey all the elements you'll need

---

(as described earlier in this section) for a positive response.

That said, in some cases this short message is all you'll need. For example, if you had an informational meeting with a potential client or hiring manager a couple of weeks ago, and all of the long emails have already been exchanged, sending a short, personal "Request to Connect" message may be an ideal way to keep yourself on their radar for opportunities that you are seeking.

Answering LinkedIn Ads

LinkedIn has a powerful feature for answering ads. It tells you who in your network is connected to the company (including the person posting the position). Here is how you take advantage of this feature.

1. Click on "Jobs" on the top menu, then "Advanced search".
2. Enter at least one or two keywords to narrow down the list of ads. Then click "Search."
3. Pick one of the numerous job postings that show up.
4. On the job posting itself, you will see either:
    a. "See people in your network who can help you get this job," meaning people in your network who are connected to the person posting the position, or
    b. "Find people in your network at <company name>," meaning they work at the company.

Use these LinkedIn features to substantially improve your odds of getting an interview; that is, don't just answer the ad. Reach out directly to the hiring manager. In one case, a client answered an ad, and then contacted the hiring manager directly via LinkedIn. The hiring manager called her the next day for an interview. The hiring manager had actually stopped looking at the ad responses (there were too many), and was close to making an offer to someone. But my client's message was so compelling that she had to interview her.

Keeping in Touch with Your Network

Leverage LinkedIn's Weekly Email Digest

Most people in your network will have arranged their settings using the default email notifications, which means that they will receive a **weekly email digest** containing their entire 1st degree network's activities. People who are highlighted in this email are those who made changes to their profile or took other actions. Be active on LinkedIn so that you show up in your network's email digest every one to three weeks—so they remember your search.

Also, review the digest to see what people in your network are up to. For example, a client looked at her weekly digest and saw that someone she worked with four years prior, and hadn't spoken to since, had been promoted (his LinkedIn job title had changed). She sent him a congratulatory note. They exchanged emails, one thing led to another, and she ended up consulting for his department!

Use "Status Updates"

On your "Home" page (click the Home menu option on top), you'll see a place where you can enter status updates. People use these updates to keep in touch with their network, as they will show up in their 1st degree connections' weekly email digests. Those who use these updates wisely consider the following:

- Post to be helpful to others, e.g. include a link to an article that may be relevant to your network.
- Post to ask for help, e.g. mention that you're trying to fill a position in your department.
- Post to let people know what you're up to, just to keep top-of-mind with your network in case they can help.
- Don't post too often—generally no more than once a day, and ideally no less than once a week. Your LinkedIn network is not the same thing as your Twitter followers, or your Facebook Page's fans. They will be turned off by dozens of posts from you in their weekly email digest, and/or the one you really want them to see may be buried by the volume.

Beth was looking for a senior level position in for-profit education on the West Coast. She decided to post a status update that read "Having numerous meetings on the West Coast to discuss senior level positions in for-profit education." One of her first degree contacts saw this update in his weekly email digest. He contacted her and connected her with someone at an organization in which she was interested, which resulted in an interview.

Joseph was a consultant, and periodically posted helpful links that reinforced his expertise in Human Resources, particularly recruiting. Someone in his first-degree network saw the posting and contacted him about a consulting position helping to identify candidates for a sales team.

How to Be Found

Don't forget to check out the section under "Getting Set-up on LinkedIn" on How to Be Found. Internal recruiters are increasingly using LinkedIn to source candidates, instead of hiring external agencies. So you want to make sure you are taking advantage of opportunities to boost your visibility in people searches.

If You're a Consultant or Own a Company

Some clients who are consultants or business owners ask me whether they should create a LinkedIn profile that reflects their company, not themselves. The answer is no. The reason: the LinkedIn profile, and the network that connects to it, is just too good a tool for **real networking** to waste this part of LinkedIn on a company promotion.

Every business owner needs a network. And when I say "real networking" I mean building and maintaining relationships over time. Don't use your profile and LinkedIn network to build a following of fans for your business—this is not a network. Instead, get a LinkedIn Company Page—this is the place to build a following on LinkedIn.

Your "Company Page"

It's very easy to set up a company page. Simply select "Companies" from the top menu, then scroll to the right where you can click "Add a Company." After that, just follow the instructions to fill out the page.

As you set up your LinkedIn company page, you'll want to send status updates to your page followers, as you do with your Facebook page feed. To do that, in the Company Page Administration section, make sure you select "Designated Users Only" and then enter your name as the designated user.

To see the potential of a company page, check out *Deloitte's* company page by searching for it in the search box on the upper right (make sure "Companies" shows in the dropdown menu to the left of the search window).

LinkedIn On-the-Job

I hope that at this point it has become apparent to you that LinkedIn is not just a tool for jobseekers. LinkedIn can be a great aid on the job as well. I deliver a seminar on the "Six Keys to On-the-Job Success." While LinkedIn can help with all of the six keys, it is particularly helpful with the two keys highlighted as follows:

✓ **Key #1: To find "Security" you need "Marketability"**
✓ Key #2: Manage Up, Down and Across
✓ Key #3: Develop a longer-term vision and a detailed plan
✓ Key #4: Know when it's time to move on
✓ **Key #5: Build and Maintain a Network**
✓ Key #6: Demonstrate Leadership

Let's take a look at each of these areas.

To find "Security" you need "Marketability"

To succeed on the job these days, you need to keep yourself and your skill set on the cutting edge. You have to think of yourself as a "consultant" for your current employer, always looking outside to bring in new value. Being an expert in anything seems more and more to be only a temporary situation. Things change quickly, and suddenly your expertise is obsolete or no longer needed. LinkedIn is a great tool for helping you to see what your "competition" is doing so that you can ensure you are maintaining your value and bringing in new ideas. Here are a few ways to do this:

- Research keywords that people use in your job target through advanced job-posting and people searches.
- Monitor or participate in LinkedIn Groups that have active discussions in your field.
- Leverage "LinkedIn Today" to get topical articles about your field delivered to your inbox.
- Follow people who are leaders in your field, within LinkedIn. Just click on "Follow" under their name and picture when you see that they have posted something in a group you share, or within "LinkedIn Today," and your weekly email status update will highlight their latest postings.

Build and Maintain a Network

As a career coach with 20 years of experience in the corporate world, it has become clear to me that relationships are 50% of career success (the other 50% being how well you can do your job). Maintaining a quality network over time is invaluable. Your network will enable you to learn about how to be best in your profession, hear about things that that may impact your job (before it's too late), hire good people, and quickly make a move within or outside of your current organization, if necessary.

Refer to the section in this book "Building Your LinkedIn Network" under "Getting Set Up" to see how to create a quality network. Also consider posing questions to your network by messaging one or more of them via LinkedIn.

Here's an example of how having a quality network helped a colleague to fill an open position.

Recruiting Using Your Network

Let's check out a real-life case study to see how you can easily use LinkedIn to help with recruiting.

> Julietta needed to hire a part-time consultant for New York University, where she was a Director. She went to "Advanced People Search" and entered keywords that related to her need, including "career services" among others. She also entered "New York University" as both a keyword and the "School," as she preferred someone who was an alum or had already done work with the school.
>
> Near the top of her list of search results, sorted by "Relevance," she found Marc, among others. He seemed to have the experience that she was looking for, as registered by the prominence of the keywords on his profile that she entered. Julietta checked out Marc's several recommendations. They looked impressive, given both the content and the levels/responsibilities of the people who recommended him.
>
> Julietta decided to reach out to him. She emailed him directly, since his email address was listed in the "Contact" section of the profile. In her note, she described the position to him, and asked if he or someone else he knew might be interested. Marc expressed his interest in the position. They met, and had a great conversation.
>
> Julietta had noticed on LinkedIn that they had a couple of mutual first degree connections whom she knew well. Julietta reached out to these mutual connections for additional reference checks. They came back strong. Julietta also found a number of other good candidates solely from her LinkedIn outreach. Some were referrals from her LinkedIn network. She ended up hiring Marc.

Using "Advanced People Search" is a great way to see if you have anyone in your network who might be able to fill a position. You may want to check with your Human Resources department, however, as they may have a paid subscription that allows them to do more sophisticated searches.

Start a Group

Starting a group within your organization can be a great way to network and collaborate with others, improving productivity. For example, I co-run the "Guild of Career Coaches" members-only group for Five O'Clock Club career coaches. Group members share advice on client challenges and the details of setting up and running individual client practices.

It is easy to set up your own LinkedIn group. Just go to "Groups" on the top menu, and select "Create a Group."

Supplement Your Organizational Intranet

If you are in a large organization, LinkedIn is a great resource for finding and reaching out to others in different departments. For example, one client worked at JP Morgan Chase, a company with over 200,000 employees. He wanted to learn about a new area of the company for a possible move down the road. Using "Advanced People Search," he found the profiles of several people at Chase that he decided to reach out to via email.

Conduct Competitor Research

To take just one example of many: A client held a senior position at a fast growing information technology cloud services company, and wanted to see how some of his slightly larger competitors organized their IT departments. He conducted advanced people searches using criteria including the competitor company name, job title, and keywords. The result: he was able to get a sense of the number of IT positions at a particular competitor, as well as the function of each position. Using this information, he was able to make the case for moving his company's hiring strategy in a new direction.

Additional Case Studies

❖ Elena was interested in working at Apple Computer as a Process Improvement manager. She conducted an "Advanced People Search" by clicking on "Advanced" next to the "People" search box on the upper right of her screen. She entered Apple as the company name, and selected "current" for currently employed at Apple. To her surprise and delight, she found that an old classmate she was connected to via a LinkedIn Group worked at Apple in a related area. She emailed him directly—and ended up eventually with an interview.

❖ Armando was searching for a senior level position directing a marketing analytics group. He conducted an "Advanced People Search" using the word "Marketing" in the job title, selecting "Current." He saw that he was indirectly connected to a Chief Marketing Officer through both a

LinkedIn Group and a mutual connection. Using the LinkedIn system he got introduced to that person through their mutual contact, and they agreed to meet. This meeting led to a series of interviews and a job offer.

❖ Janis was interested in researching the field of Organizational Development. She joined a Group called the "Organizational Development Network." This Group's discussions were lively and informative. She was able to get answers to a range of questions, and contributed to the discussions where she could. New contacts she made via the Group led to several informational meetings.

❖ David was in retail store sales management. He was looking to meet a senior executive in a top New York luxury retail outlet where he wanted to work. Through an advanced people search, he found the name of the person he wanted to reach. He saw that they shared both a group and a mutual connection. David messaged this executive through the group, using the guidelines specified in the "Messaging via a Group" section of this chapter. 13 minutes later (according to his happy email to me), he received a reply agreeing to a meeting for an exploratory interview (which ultimately led to a job offer).

❖ Nina was interested in working at a Hedge Fund specializing in "Alternative Investments," but she had no idea which firms to target. She clicked on "Companies" (under "Interests") then "Search Companies." She typed "Alternative Investments" in the company search window at the top, and got thousands of entries. She narrowed down her list to a much more manageable 60 or so firms by selecting Industry ("investment management"), Geography, and then Company Size from the options listed in the left column of the page.

LinkedIn's Paid Services

Since the free features in LinkedIn are so useful for your job search, don't sign up for the paid services right away. Use them if you feel you have maxed-out on LinkedIn's free features. LinkedIn offers different packages of paid services. For example, its "JobSeeker" packages currently cost from $20 to $50 per month. I'll note three of the more useful features:

- You can send a limited number of "InMails." This feature allows you to message anyone in LinkedIn, whether you are connected to them or not.
- You can request more introductions per month beyond those that come with your free account.
- Your profile is pushed higher up the list when recruiters do candidate searches by keyword.

Common Concerns and Questions about LinkedIn

People unfamiliar with LinkedIn often raise these concerns to me. Here are my answers.

"My Boss Will Know I'm Looking"

Your boss will not see that you are asking for introductions and contacting people in groups. As far as other updates to your Profile, the mere fact that you are active on LinkedIn should not mean to your boss or anyone else that you are necessarily looking for a job. Many people (including myself) use LinkedIn to enhance success in their current positions. In addition, it is certainly advisable that everyone, your boss included, keep up with their network via LinkedIn.

That said, LinkedIn can be a challenge if you are trying to make a career change without your boss knowing. Your boss could become suspicious if your profile reflects a different profession than your current one. My advice: instead of a targeted profile that speaks just to employers in your new career, have a broader profile that encompasses both your current position and your new career direction.

For example, I had a client who was interested in moving from business-development in information technology to financial analysis. So his profile positioned himself broadly, as a "Finance and IT professional with broad experience including financial analysis, business development, and IT."

Note that I advise a more focused, targeted approach for your resume and pitch. The reason: you can only have one profile, that's visible to your entire network (you can't pick and choose, it's either your entire network or no one), while you can and should have a different resume for each job target.

"I don't want some people to know I'm changing my profile"

Occasionally someone asks me whether there is a way to selectively prevent certain people from being notified about profile updates. You cannot prevent notifying select individuals, but you can prevent notifications to your entire network. Select "Settings" from the dropdown menu by your name, in the upper right corner of the screen. Under "Privacy Controls," select "**Turn on/off Your Activity Broadcasts**" and uncheck the box.

"I don't want all of my information out there for anyone to see"

As mentioned previously, you can alter your settings to make them visible to different groups of people, from everyone to just your 1st degree network (or to no one at all). I would advise at the very least having your profile visible to the people you connect with. Also, there is no need to fill out the "Personal Information" section of your profile.

"Shouldn't I only connect with people in my profession?"

The answer is no. You never know who knows someone who knows someone. Recently a client who's job target was "financial analyst" landed a coveted interview because she had connected with her next door neighbor, with whom she had a distant but friendly relationship. It turns out that the neighbor's husband's brother-in-law knew the CFO at a company she was targeting, and put her in touch.

If you've been reading this guide straight through, you're probably tuckered out and in need of a break by now!   So here's a good place to rest.

3. EMAIL LISTS

"I get mail; therefore I am."
Scott Adams

> **In this Chapter:**
> ✓ Many associations have active, thoughtful email lists that cover hot-topics in your field. If so, you should take advantage of this important benefit.
> ✓ Search email "conversations" in list archives to learn more about your profession.
> ✓ Ask questions of other colleagues on the list that can help you with your search.
> ✓ Answer questions posed by list colleagues, to help build your reputation.

Email Lists (also referred to as electronic mailing lists, or sometimes incorrectly as *Listserves*) are a tool for sharing messages among individuals who subscribe to the list that form conversations around specific topics. These conversations can be archived and are searchable. You do not need any special software to subscribe to an email list.

These lists can be useful for your job search. Messages can be created, viewed, and replied to via your email inbox or online through the site that hosts the messages. Many of the most useful email lists are offshoots of professional associations that you already (or will) belong to, as part of your approach to getting interviews. Below are two examples from my own experience.

MENG, or the Marketing Executives Networking Group (www.mengonline.org), an organization that I belong to, has an email list set up that can be viewed from its website, or via messages received in your email inbox. There are strict rules for the types of messages that can be sent. Moderated email lists, such as this one, facilitate the most interesting, useful discussions.

One of the formats on the MENG email list allows you to start certain messages with [Requests], meaning you want to ask the members for information. I had a client who used this format to ask the membership if they knew how to approach a particular person or people at a large multinational company. This request garnered many responses, one of which led to an interview.

The second example: the Organizational Development Network (ODN) (www.odnetwork.org) has a very active email list with professionals who are devoted in helping each other to advance in their careers and share learning. To give you an idea of the quality of the discussions on a good email list, I went to the ODN's website and skimmed the most recent archives, and immediately saw substantial discussions on the following topics:

- What OD Blogs do you read?
- Distinguishing between OD and Training
- HR and OD

You can see how participating in email lists can help you. They enable learning by reading the discussions, asking questions, and contributing your own valuable comments and insights, which will serve to impress prospective employers.

Note: Before posting on an email list, observe the etiquette of the posts and use a similar style yourself. In addition, if you can, be proactive in answering your colleagues' questions. This is an effective way to market yourself; you are more likely to get the help you are looking for in return.

4. TWITTER

"Somewhere, something incredible is waiting to be known."
Carl Sagan

In this Chapter:
- ✓ Twitter can be VERY helpful for job-target research.
- ✓ It can also be helpful for getting interviews via tweeting to those who you follow.
- ✓ Twitter's job search benefit is NOT primarily from building a following for your tweets.
- ✓ Twitter works well for certain professions, but not for others.
- ✓ You need to invest three or four hours experimenting with Twitter to see if it will work well for your job target.
- ✓ Given this time investment and uncertain payoff, place Twitter further down on your list of things to do, and well-below getting set-up on LinkedIn.
- ✓ You need a free "Twitter Organizer" to use Twitter for your job search.
- ✓ Finding people and "lists" to follow often involves going outside of Twitter, to external websites where directories of Twitter users are housed.

What Is Twitter?

Twitter is a free service that enables its users to send and read messages known as *tweets*. These are messages of up to 140 characters that are displayed on the author's profile page and delivered to the author's subscribers who are known as *followers*. All users can send and receive tweets via the Twitter website or external applications.

Some people use Twitter to build a following via their tweets. Others use Twitter primarily to search for information or respond occasionally to the tweets of others to build relationships.

Caution: Tweeting to build a following can be time-consuming and the payoff uncertain. Although you may get results for your job search eventually, for most searches I believe there are better ways to spend your time. Using

Twitter for research and to build relationships, on the other hand, could hold substantial benefits for your job search, depending on your field or profession.

Who should be on Twitter?

Whether you should be on Twitter depends a lot on the nature of your job target. Some targets lend themselves to doing research and building relationships via Twitter, others don't.

Twitter works best with job targets that can be easily identified using certain keywords as search terms. For example, "marketing," "supply chain," "retail supply chain," "biotechnology," and "green tech" all work well with Twitter, because these simple words describe distinct practices and groups of people who have something to offer in these specialties.

On the other hand, if you only use the keywords "sales," "retail sales," or "finance" to describe your target, Twitter may be less useful to you. These terms are too broad, requiring too much precious job-search time to sift through and find useful posts. "Sales" may turn up tweets from people trying to sell you something, rather than, for instance, people sharing knowledge about industry buyers in your field. "Finance" may generate tweets from people who want to be your personal financial advisor, when you're really looking for people who cover the latest issues in international corporate finance, in your search for a Finance Department VP job.

In addition, it _may_ be that people in certain professions have a greater presence on Twitter than others. For example, the "social," "communication," and "tech-related" professions seem to gravitate toward Twitter, including information technology, marketing, sales, public relations, and entrepreneurs (including performing artists).

For those job targets that are easily described and well represented, Twitter can be VERY helpful in advancing your job search. My advice: After you have picked the low-hanging fruit in your job search, **spend three or four hours investigating Twitter to see if you can apply its unique features and benefits to your job target**. If, after this time, you are feeling frustrated, then stop trying to make it work and move on to something else.

How Twitter Can Help Your Job Search
Twitter can be most helpful for:
- **Research**. Think of Twitter as a search portal for quickly and easily accessing the most up-to-date, relevant information for your job target.

- o   Learn from leaders in your field about the latest developments, or what they are thinking and reading, nearly as fast as they are thinking or reading it!

- o   Set up Twitter to make it far easier than conducting Google searches to identify and access the information you need for your job target and company research.

- **Relationship-building**. Follow people you don't know (or those you do know) to possibly build or strengthen a professional relationship with them that could lead to referrals and interviews. You can comment on the tweets of others, and start a dialogue with people you would otherwise not have access to.

- **Getting the word out about your search**. If you can get someone with thousands of followers to tweet the thing you need— a job, for example—that can be powerful! You may be able to accomplish this through relationships you build on Twitter, or just through asking someone you know in the "real world" with a following to tweet your job search.

Getting Set-up on Twitter

Go to www.twitter.com and get your free User ID and password. For job search marketing purposes, try to have your full name comprise all or part of your User ID.[4]

Next you will need a free **Social Media Dashboard,** the filing system for tweets, to organize your tweets by job target, company, and the ways you are searching within each job target. Dashboards make it easy to spot useful information, and are essential when using Twitter for your job search.

Twitter dashboards/organizers allow you to group tweets into columns defined by you—for example, you can have a company column or an industry column. You will need a separate user id and password for your organizer. Once it is set up, you will rarely need to go to your twitter.com home page.

These organizers can be located on your desktop or online. Popular organizers include *Tweetdeck*, and *Hootsuite* (and there are others). For demonstration purposes, I'll reference Hootsuite.

---

[4] The concept is similar with your email address. If you have doggie23@hotmail.com as your primary email address, get a new one just for your job search with your full name in it, like janisjoplin@hotmail.com.

Terms You Need to Know

Here are some of the basic terms you will come across when using Twitter through Hootsuite.

- **Lists:** These are compiled by Twitter users (anyone can create a public or private list), and group together people tweeting on a particular topic. The advantage of lists is that you can get all the tweets at once from individuals on the list—you don't have to follow each individual. One example of the many thousands of public lists people have put together is "CTO", that is, a list of corporate Chief Technology Officers who tweet.

- **Stream:** a column of tweets in Hootsuite that is generated by either search terms or the name of a Twitter list. All tweets in Hootsuite are separated into individual streams/columns. There are four types of streams:
  - **Feed:** a stream of all the tweets you have received or sent.
  - **Keyword:** a stream of tweets based on an individual keyword search.
  - **Search:** columns containing tweets filtered by phrases. You can use AND/OR connectors as well, such as "Merck AND Pfizer."
  - **Lists:** a stream that contains a public Twitter list you are following, or a list of tweeters that you are compiling yourself (public or private).

- **Tab:** A "filing cabinet" on Hootsuite that contains up to 10 streams.

- **Link Shorteners:** Website links can often be long. Since tweets are no longer than 140 characters, website link-shrinking is essential. Most Twitter organizers can shrink your links for you if you enter the full link on the top of the screen (where you would tweet) and click "Shrink It." Online services such as http://ow.ly/url/shorten-url can also shrink your links for you.

- **Re-tweet, or RT:** This is a convention for "re-tweet." If you are passing on the information from someone else's tweet, it is common courtesy to add RT, and the username, within the tweet you are forwarding (that is, re-tweeting).

- **@username:** the @ sign signifies the Twitter name of the person. For me it would be @robhellmann. So, you might see "RT @robhellmann" followed by the tweet content.

- **Hashtags:** these reference the "#" character, as in #jobs, #marketing, etc. They signify user-created topics that catch on with a lot of users, and become conventions for searching by topic. For example, someone long ago (e.g., three years ago) decided that #jobs would mean tweets that link to job postings, and this convention caught on. See the Twitter resource links in the Appendix for popular hashtags.

Organizing Your Tweets using a "Dashboard"

Go to www.hootsuite.com, and get a free logon ID and password. Below you will find specifics on how to use Hootsuite, but first review Hootsuite's "help" resources, by clicking on the "Help" link at the bottom of its home page (or go directly to http://help.hootsuite.com/home). Also helpful is Twitter's support page at http://support.twitter.com/ .

Use a two-step approach to find relevant tweeters and organize their tweets.

1. **Search terms:** Set up separate streams of tweets within Hootsuite based on Twitter search terms. For example, you can set up search terms for company names, industries, or professions, and have separate streams of tweets for each of these.

2. **External websites:** Twitter is not a self-contained platform the way LinkedIn is. To really use Twitter effectively, you need to go beyond twitter.com and your Twitter dashboard/organizer to make use of external sites. These websites help to identify tweeters to follow by categorizing tweeters according to profession, industry, workplace, interest and popularity. You can find both individual tweeters as well as public "lists" of tweeters to follow.

   Wefollow (www.wefollow.com) is a good website for finding both lists and individuals to follow (other sites are listed in the Appendix). We will use this website as an example. Once you set yourself up to follow an individual via Wefollow, you would go back to Hootsuite to place the individual in the proper section of your organizer.

Using Twitter

A Case Study

Let's use a client's job search to illustrate how Twitter can help you with yours. Sarah's primary job target is Marketing Director for pharmaceutical companies in the Northeastern U.S. The top two companies she is targeting are Merck and Pfizer. Sarah wants Twitter to help her with:

- **Company Research:** Keeping current with the latest developments at Merck and Pfizer so that Sarah can use this information to get and ace interviews.

- **Research on Job Targets:** Keeping current on the latest trends in marketing in general, and pharma marketing in particular.
- **Networking:** Finding interesting or useful links that she can send to selected people in her network, as a way of keeping in touch with them (e.g., someone she interviewed with a month ago for a position that may still be open). Also, develop and maintain relationships with people in a position to refer her, give advice, or hire her.
- **Making New Connections:** Contacting people at Merck or Pfizer whom she doesn't know in order to build relationships, which may lead to interviews.

Sarah sees Twitter as a way to 1) find valuable information that she might not have known about otherwise, 2) access information that she could have found elsewhere, but in a faster, easier way, on an ongoing basis, and 3) develop relationships helpful to her search that she might otherwise not have had an opportunity to develop.

Setting Up Twitter Search Streams

Sarah signed up for Twitter and Hootsuite, and viewed the Hootsuite help links. She then spent an hour experimenting with the correct search terms and keywords for setting up her initial streams (i.e. columns). On Hootsuite, Sarah clicked on the "add stream" button near the upper left and saw a new dialog box with four column-type choices, including "Feed", "Search", "Keyword" and "Lists" (picture that follows).

The dialog box also contains options to receive streams from many different social media sources, not just Twitter. Sarah made sure that "Twitter" was selected.

Sarah set up the following five columns (or streams):

1) A Keyword column that searched the word "Pfizer" for Pfizer's latest developments.
2) A Search column that searched the words "Pfizer Marketing" (meaning any tweet that contains both of the words "Pfizer" and "Marketing" within the tweet) for current news about Pfizer's marketing initiatives.
3) A Keyword column that searched the word "Merck."
4) A Search column that searched the words "Merck Marketing."
5) A Search column for "Pharma Marketing" for up-to-date marketing information on the pharmaceutical industry.

The picture below shows how columns 3, 4 and 5 look. Let's explore each one to see what Sarah has learned so far from her efforts.

The picture that follows is a zoomed-in excerpt of the picture above.

Keyword column "Merck"
In this column, Sarah immediately spotted a few interesting tweets. These included:
- Several tweets about Merck's quarterly results.
- Critical overview of Merck's product pipeline.
- Numerous employment opportunity postings from "MerckJobs."

Search column "Merck Marketing"
The results, though similar to the "Merck" Keyword column, included additional useful tweets. For example: Merck's acquisition of the marketing rights for a new product.

Search column "Pharma Marketing"
Sarah found several tweets giving her useful information about her target industry. The tweets included links to articles on:
- Growth prospects for the pharma industry
- Marketing analytics and pharma
- Pharma's branding

In one tweet, she also found a reference to a pharma marketing blog that she subscribed to, which was a valuable source for the latest industry gossip and information In addition to the articles themselves, the tweets gave her links to new resources. For example, Sarah clicked on the link for Sigma_MG, the tweeter of the "Marketing Analytics and Pharma" article, and saw this:

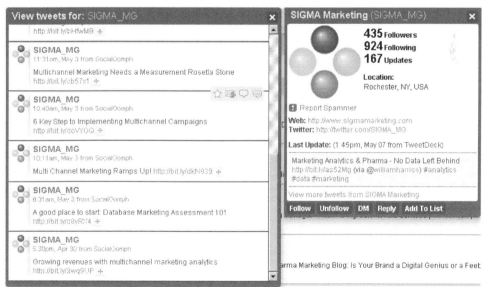

Since Sarah found these tweets to be helpful to her job search, she decided to follow SIGMA_MG, by clicking on "Follow" at the bottom right. She then

---

created a new stream in Hootsuite, selected "lists" as the column type, called the column "Tweeters in Pharma Marketing," and added SIGMA_MG as the first member to this list.

Searching External Websites for Individuals and Lists to Follow

Sarah found individuals to follow by going to www.wefollow.com. Once she found a person or list she wanted to follow on Wefollow, she would click "follow" and then jump back to the Hootsuite organizer to "file" and properly label the person. She would then go back to Wefollow to search for more people and repeat the process. She also looked at the lists that these individuals followed, and chose to subscribe to some of them as well. Here are the specific steps Sarah took.

1) On Wefollow, she entered "Pharm" in the "**Search by interest**" box on top of the Home page, and selected "Pharma" from the dropdown. The search results included individual tweeters sorted by their "Prominence" score (roughly based on the number of follwers who are engaged "listeners" with their own followings). Within the results, Sarah noticed the tweeter "Pharmagossip," clicked on the name, and found some useful tweets from Merck's CEO about the industry and her target companies.

2) Sarah decided to follow Pharmagossip. She did this by clicking on the "Pharmagossip" link, then on "Follow…"

3) She then went to Hootsuite to add Pharmagossip to her "Tweeters in Pharma Marketing" list. The picture that follows illustrates Sarah's four steps to add Pharmagossip.

A. Click on the little house icon in Hootsuite, in the upper left corner.
B. Select "Contacts" from the dropdown menu.
C. Select "People I Follow".
D. Hover over the thumbnail of their picture, then drag over to your list and let go of the mouse.

4) Sarah went back to Wefollow and then repeated this process to add some other tweeters to her "Tweeters in Pharma Marketing" list (including official company tweeters from Pfizer and other companies she is interested in).

5) She now tried a new search on Wefollow, entering "Pharma Marketing" instead of just "Pharma" in the Search People box. She found additional people she wanted to follow, and added them to her Pharma Marketing list in Hootsuite.

6) Sarah continued with her trial and error approach to finding people and lists to follow. She now entered "Pfizer" in the People search, and quickly found the name of a Technology Director in Marketing. She decided to follow this person, as someone who may be able to help her with her search in Pfizer.

Making New Connections: Sarah noticed one of the Director's posts that she wanted to reply to, just a generic post about having a hard day. So Sarah went to the post, and clicked on the "Direct Message" icon to right of the tweet to send a personal message that only the tweeter would see.

7) Sarah was pleasantly surprised when she quickly got an appreciative response. She knew she would want to keep in touch via Twitter, in the hopes of leveraging this contact for an informational meeting or additional introductions to others in the company.

8) Next, Sarah decided to search for whole Lists that she might want to follow. She noticed that Pharmagossip followed a public list called "Pharm" that contained 19 Twitterers. She liked the results, so she decided to follow this list as well (by clicking on "Subscribe").

9) Now back on Hootsuite, she decided to create a new "Sarah lists" tab just for the lists she was following, while keeping her search columns in the "Sarah" tab. She did this by clicking on the "+" button to the right of the tabs, and then adding "Sarah lists". She then clicked on the "+Add Stream" icon on the upper left, selected "lists", and picked the "Pharma/biotech" list she just subscribed to from the dropdown menu.

10) For one last check, Sarah went back to the main Twitter home page, to see if Twitter might make additional suggestions on who to follow, now that she was following a few people and lists. She clicked on "Who to Follow" on the left column, and decided to follow some of the suggestions offered.

Conclusion: In three hours Sarah succeeded in setting up a system on Twitter that would accomplish her objectives of 1) learning new, valuable information she wouldn't have known about, 2) accessing information more easily, and 3) developing new professional relationships.

Sarah's example should demonstrate how you can use Twitter to advance your job search. As you can see, experimentation and effort are required to find the correct search terms for your job target, and people or lists to follow.

Careful: Look before you Tweet!
If you tweet to your followers or reply to a tweet, remember that once you press "Send-Now" everyone can see your post! If you mean to send a private message, make sure you hit the "Direct Message" button, and not "Reply".

You can, however, delete an errant tweet so that it will disappear from your followers' feeds and search engines.
Here's what you do:

1. Log in to Twitter at www.twitter.com.
2. Visit your profile.
3. Locate the tweet that you want to delete.

4. Click the trash can on the lower right corner of
    the tweet.

Deleted tweets sometimes linger in Twitter search. They will clear with time.

An Errant Tweet

5. BLOGS

"If you can't explain it simply, you don't understand it well enough."
Albert Einstein

In this Chapter:
✓ Follow the blogs of leaders in your field to learn about the latest developments that will help you land and ace interviews.

✓ Consider using the "comments" section of a blog to establish a dialogue with a blogger who may be able to help you with your search.

✓ Don't blog regularly for your job-search unless it really comes easily to you.

✓ Do consider writing an occasional blog entry to demonstrate your expertise and currency in your field.

What is a Blog?
A blog is "a type of website, usually maintained by an individual with regular entries of commentary, descriptions of events, or other material such as graphics or video." *(Wikipedia)*

Blogs enable anyone to become writers, journalists, or publishers. There are several free sites that allow you to quickly get started with blogging, including www.blogger.com and www.wordpress.com.

Blogs are commonly incorporated into existing websites, as mine is. You can use blogs to help your job search by:
• Writing your own blog
• Reading other people's blogs
• Commenting on other people's blogs

Writing Your Own Blog
Bloggers usually want to draw attention to their blog and build a following, which means they have to update their blog at least once a week (and often several times a day!). Do not seek to write and update a blog this often, unless blogging comes very easily to you, or your job target involves writing your opinions frequently and under deadline. There are better ways to spend

your valuable job-search time.

You may want to write just one or two blog entries, however, or just update your blog occasionally (say once a month). You will not be building a following this way, but you can use these infrequent entries to show that you are current and knowledgeable in your field. Consider this approach if:

- You have been out of work for a while.
- You are seeking to make a career or industry change.
- The knowledge needed for success in your field is changing rapidly.

One of my clients began a blog in her field: Supply Chain Management. She wrote just one entry to demonstrate that she is current in her field. She wrote about new Federal regulations and how they would impact supply chain managers. Her blog, which included her email signature and LinkedIn profile address, caught the attention of hiring managers at a company she was applying to work in, and ultimately led to a job offer. The hiring managers said that this one blog entry played a critical role in their decision-making.

Naming Your Blog

If you do decide to write your own blog, have your name in the blog website address to most effectively market yourself. (WordPress will give you instructions on how to do that as you register). The job search is about marketing yourself, and your name is the name of "your product."

Reading Other People's Blogs

Subscribe to blogs that can help you to research your target, including companies where you would like to work.

One place to find relevant blogs is at http://technorati.com/blogs/directory/. This website lists the top most referenced blogs, by category. You will quickly see that this particular site is useful for some fields (Entertainment and Personal Finance), but not for others, such as Marketing. Another way to search is by going to blogsearch.google.com, but it will take you a lot of time to wade through all of your search results, and you may still not find what you are looking for.

So, how do you quickly find the best blogs to follow for your job target? I always advocate starting with the obvious, easy things first. For example, I googled "Best Marketing blog" and within five minutes identified top blogs and useful information that would be very helpful in generating interviews for a marketing position.

Another great way to find the best blogs is by asking professionals in your profession or industry what they read. Use your LinkedIn groups, LinkedIn "Answers", or associations you are affiliated with to ask these questions. Or, see what blogs people in your field are tweeting about.

Replying to the Blogs of Others
When you follow the blogs of leaders in your field, engage them in an intelligent, appropriate way, via leaving blog "comments". Start online conversations that could perhaps lead to building new professional relationships.

Keeping Track of the Blogs You Follow with "Feed Readers"
You may have noticed that most blogs and many news sites display an orange icon that looks like this: This "RSS feed" icon indicates that the content is available for inclusion in a "feed reader." This web application makes it very easy to scan a large number of blogs and news reports quickly for information that interests you. Readers are one of the best ways of keeping on top of the voluminous information that is available to you as you research job targets and prepare for interviews.

One of the most popular feed readers is "Google Reader." You will need a free account with Google to access the reader (if you have a Gmail account, you can use that). Go to http://reader.google.com to sign up. Important: You will need to take the additional step of going to www.feedly.com and opening a Reader account there as well, before July 1st, 2013. To continue using Google Reader feeds after that, you will have to go through Feedly, as Google Reader is shutting down and Feedly is migrating Google Reader users to its site.

Once you have your account set up, go to a blog or news source that displays the RSS feed icon, and click on it. You will then see a list of icons representing various readers. Here's an example:

Click on the "Google" icon to add this feed to the Google Reader. You can then sign into the reader and see the feed displayed. You can create folders in the reader and sort and organize your feeds for easy browsing.

I follow a lot of career management and workplace blogs, and I organize those in a folder I call "Career Services News." As you can see from the picture, I can skim through the titles and descriptions to find posts that look interesting. I can then click on interesting items to read them. Frequently they can be read within the reader itself—that is, you don't have to open a ton of web pages as you read through the posts. An excerpt from my reader follows.

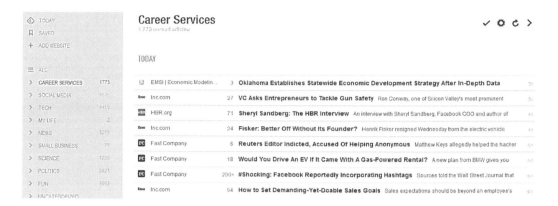

Feedly will also suggest popular feeds that are similar to those you subscribe to, as another way of identifying blogs involving your job target.

And of course, you can always follow my (sporadic) blog posts in your feed reader by going to my www.hellmannconsulting.com home page and clicking on the orange RSS feed icon.

The first blog

6. FACEBOOK

"It's a small world, but we all run in big circles."
Sasha Azevedo

In this Chapter:
✓ Facebook is primarily social by nature, which makes it less useful for your job search—it is not a substitute for LinkedIn!

✓ If you already have a substantial network on Facebook, use it to let your network know about your search.

✓ If you are not already a heavy user of Facebook, do not invest time with this platform just for your job search.

✓ Facebook's integration with a job-board aggregator can help you reach the hiring manager who is filling a position via an online ad.

✓ Facebook fan pages can be very useful in building a business or an audience.

Facebook now has over 1 billion users. Go to www.facebook.com to sign up for this free service. Facebook allows users to add people as "friends," in order to send them messages and updates on their personal profiles. Additionally, users can join networks organized by workplace, school, or profession.

If you do not use Facebook regularly, then I don't recommend immersing yourself more deeply in it just for the job search. Because Facebook's primary use is social in nature (as opposed to professional), it is often not good etiquette to contact someone you don't really know about target research or an informational meeting. It could be off-putting. In addition, if you have been using Facebook for maintaining contact with close friends and family, it will feel inappropriate to all parties involved (including your new business "friends") to start bringing business contacts into this circle. **LinkedIn is the place to do this kind of professional outreach.**

If you are already on Facebook, however, and are using it actively to keep in touch with people, then use Facebook to tell your network of Facebook "friends" about your search. In that context, Facebook could be very useful for letting your network know how they can help you. Also, take a look at Facebook groups, described next.

Facebook Groups

These groups are similar to LinkedIn groups in that they are a place for

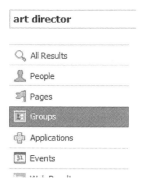

registered users who share a particular interest, profession, or association. They are not as tailored, however, as LinkedIn groups are for the job search. Nevertheless, they could place you in a community that could help you build new career-advancing relationships.

Here's how you find and join a Facebook group. Log into Facebook and go to the search box on top. Type in "Art Director" for example (or whatever other phrase represents your job target). Before you press enter, scroll down past the "top 3 results" that automatically appear, and click on "see more results for Art Director." You will initially see all results that contain the words "art director", not just results for groups. To see just the groups, select "Groups" from the left column (see picture that follows):

Once you have selected to see only groups, you can then narrow down the list further by interest, by using the Type and Subtype menus:

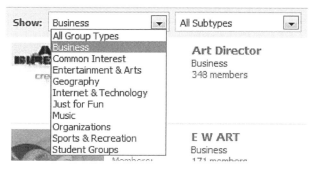

Just to illustrate one example of the difference between Facebook groups and LinkedIn groups, you can try typing in "Art Director" yourself on the group searches of both applications. You will immediately be struck by the differences in group quality for "Art Director" between the two applications: the LinkedIn groups for Art Director have far more members and more current, active useful discussions on the profession. My own research, and the feedback I receive from clients, suggests that LinkedIn generally has more and better business-networking oriented groups.

Facebook Integration with www.Simplyhired.com

Simply Hired is an aggregator of online job-boards (like www.indeed.com) that enables you to avoid having to search through multiple websites for ads.

If you scroll down Simply Hired's home page, you will see a "Facebook" icon. Click on it, follow the instructions and you will then be able to see which of your Facebook friends works at the company posting an ad. This useful feature (and the equivalent feature on LinkedIn) can help you get right to the hiring manager, thereby obtaining a crucial leg-up on applicants who are only applying via the ad.

Facebook Pages

One final thought: Facebook can potentially be very helpful if you are trying to build a business or an audience for events, provided that a significant segment of your potential customers tend to also be on Facebook. You can attract attention to your business by setting up a "Fan Page" that could drive traffic to your business. I know of clients and colleagues that have done very well advertising their events or attracting new customers via these fan pages. See Section 8 for more information on Facebook pages and building a business.

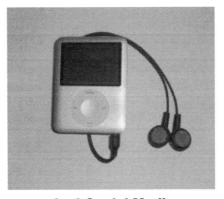

Anti-Social Media

7. JOB SEARCH CASE STUDY: USING LIMITED TIME WISELY

"Do first things first, and second things not at all."
Peter Drucker

John was a business analyst interested in moving from Financial Services to the administrative side of a university in his area. He did not, however, know much about how universities could use his business analysis background, nor did he know anyone who worked at any of the universities he was interested in. So, did he run right to Twitter or start a blog? No! Here's what he did, in the following order:

1) **Alumni Associations:** John first used both his undergraduate and graduate school alumni network to see if anyone worked at the universities on his list. Both schools had an easily searchable online database that allowed him to find names of people to reach out to in his job target.

   He then emailed and phoned them to ask for 20-minute informational meetings to discuss a) how he might use his skills in a university setting, and b) who else they thought he should connect with. This was a highly successful approach; it enabled him to create his pitch about how he could help universities, and also gave him a couple of contact names.

2) **LinkedIn Profile:** As John gathered this initial information, he used it to revise his resume and his LinkedIn profile, to make him appear more of an "insider." John wanted to use the right keywords in his Summary Section that would help him to be found by recruiters. Given that he was making an industry change, however, he knew that he would not be the ideal candidate for recruiters, and would have to rely even more on networking and making new connections.

3) **LinkedIn Introductions:** Now that John had an effective LinkedIn profile, he looked at his LinkedIn network. John found that he had several 2nd degree contacts at universities where he wanted to work. He reached out to his 1st degree contacts to get the introductions.

   When asking for introductions, John made it clear that he would not be asking for a job. Instead, he asked for a brief, mutually beneficial conversation about how his skill set could be useful to a university down the road. His introduction requests were accepted.

4) **Making new connections via LinkedIn Groups:** John also noticed a

couple of contacts at universities in his target area where they shared only a common LinkedIn group. John messaged these contacts directly through the LinkedIn system. In his message, he:

    a. Made it clear he wasn't asking for a job, but rather an informational meeting.
    b. Found a way to say the meeting could be mutually beneficial.
    c. Asked for only 20 minutes of their time.
    d. Included his pitch, in which he emphasized how his skills might benefit a university down the road.

5) **Updates to LinkedIn Network:** John also began keeping his LinkedIn network updated on his activities. In one instance, he used the "Answers" feature to answer a question about how to analyze donor information to increase university fundraising opportunities. This answer showed up in the weekly email digest his 1st degree network received. One 1st degree contact who saw his answer sent him this message: "I didn't know you had this kind of expertise! You should really talk to a client of mine; he would be interested in your background." This exchange resulted in an informational interview, which in turn led to an interview for a new position.

6) **Updates to his Remaining Network:** John thought broadly about his network and included his friends and family, his former colleagues from 10 years ago, and a former teacher. He surprised himself by coming up with close to 200 names!

He then contacted these 200 people to ask for their help in making contacts at universities he was focusing on. He did this in two ways. 1) He sent out a mass email to all those he had an email address for. 2) He also was very active on Facebook, so he sent the same message out to all of his Facebook "friends." John got numerous responses this way, with some very productive leads.

7) **Industry Publications:** John did a search on some online journals for articles that could give him more background on both his target universities and on people to contact. In one, the *Chronicle of Higher Education*, he found two relevant articles written by well-placed administrators in target universities.

He contacted both by email, introduced himself, referenced their respective articles, included his pitch, and requested a meeting not to ask for a job, but to have a mutually beneficial discussion. He got meetings with both of them that eventually led to interviews.

8) **Professional Association:** John joined "CASE," an association focused on university Advancement, an area he felt his business analysis expertise could help in. It cost him around $80 for the year,

but was well worth the investment. He found an abundance of articles online that gave him greater insight into how he could help potential employers.

9) **Email list:** John began participating in the CASE email list, and over time began building up additional contacts that gave him more of an insider status.

10) **Looking Like an Insider:** By now John had a robust search going on. He had many leads into the universities and colleges he was interested in. His initial conversations with alumni helped him figure out how to sell his skills to those who might be in a position to hire him in his job target. Now two months into his search, he was having six concurrent conversations with people who were in a position to hire him.

11) **Preparing for Interviews:** To prepare for his interviews John set up "Google Alerts" for the key universities he was targeting, so that he could keep on top of the latest news for his job target.[5]

12) **Experimenting with Twitter:** John also decided to help prepare for interviews by checking out Twitter. John spent about three hours researching Twitter to see if there was any potential for him to use this platform.

First, he tried searching for Twitter users to follow on Wefollow. John found, however, that none of the users he uncovered were really worth following, as the tweets reflected mainly on-campus student activities. Then John went to Hootsuite and tried creating search columns for the universities he was targeting. He found that their tweets were mostly targeted to on-campus activities as well.

John ultimately created two columns on Hootsuite that did turn up relevant tweets, involving the keywords "fundraising advancement" and "university tuition". He decided, however, that it would be easier to access the tweets in these search columns via LinkedIn's *Company Buzz* application; he wouldn't have to keep opening a separate Twitter application. John decided he had spent enough time investigating Twitter and would rely on LinkedIn for Twitter information he needed.

13) **Blog:** John considered starting a blog and writing just one or two entries, to further demonstrate his expertise in business analysis as it pertains to university advancement. But the success he was having with his search made blogging an extra effort that he felt was unnecessary. He did begin keeping track of college Advancement

---

[5] He did this by a) going to news.google.com, doing a keyword search, then if he liked the results, scrolling to the bottom and selecting "Create an email alert."

blogs on Google Reader that he found out about through the CASE email list.

14) **Tweeting:** John didn't really consider tweeting, because he felt the time was not worth the effort. He was already getting strong positive results from his other methods.

Over a three-month period, while still working full-time at his financial services job, John managed through this effort to obtain several interviews for positions he was interested in. He had to juggle multiple job offers, finally accepting an offer that he was very interested in.

John's results demonstrate how online social media can combine with more traditional approaches to create a highly successful job search. May you too achieve success in your search!

8. SOCIAL MEDIA FOR BUILDING A BUSINESS

"Your time is limited, so don't waste it living someone else's life."
Steve Jobs

More and more, I'm seeing jobseekers who are considering starting their own business as an interim or long-term solution to elusive income security. Many of you may already be in business for yourselves as consultants. Given this trend, I thought it would be helpful to include some thoughts on how social media can help to grow your business.

Before jumping into how social media can help market your business, however, let's consider how social media should fit into your overall marketing priorities. Doing social media right for your business is time consuming! Recently I heard a talk by Michael Porter, who is well known for his books and seminars on marketing your business. He said that very small businesses with limited time and resources should focus primarily on one of three marketing channels, and not try to do it all:

- Giving Talks
- Writing
- Social Media

I've found this rule of thumb to be valuable for my own business. Also, consider the nature of your business and what your target audience would respond to. Maybe old fashioned email would work best. Or, perhaps your brick and mortar business is so local that the wide geographic reach of many social media platforms would not be a benefit. On the other hand, "FourSquare," a social media platform that encourages traffic to brick and mortar businesses, might be just the thing. "Pinterest" is another social media platform that is worth a look if your product or service is visual in nature (e.g. graphic design, photography, etc.).

Building a Following

One way that social media is commonly used in business-building is by leveraging its ability to help you develop a following for your products or services (the other way is by reaching out one-on-one). Successful social media initiatives for business have involved followings of hundreds, thousands or even millions of people. I've seen clients and colleagues use their large followings to fill their events, increase usage of their services, and publicize new product launches. Here are a few quick examples:

- ❖ A colleague of mine fills all of her career services classes via status updates to her thousands of Facebook Page followers.

- ❖ My sporadic blog posts have still been enough to bring in substantial new business, including several paid speaking engagements, media opportunities, and new clients.

- ❖ A book published in 2012 achieved #1 ranking on both Amazon and Barnes & Noble in **June of 2011, while the author was still writing it**! How? He tweeted about the book to his 1.1 million Twitter followers, and also shared it on some smaller online communities.[6]

The key to success in developing an engaged following is to add real value, with sincerity, in your social media interactions. Share useful links, solid advice, or promotions and discounts. Or be very witty.

Here are some high level thoughts on how each of the applications we discussed in this book can help you.

Facebook

This platform works very well for building a following because of its enormous user base and features for posting to followers. You will need to set up a Facebook business "Page" in addition to your personal page. A Facebook Page is a Facebook-specific website for your business. These pages are becoming fairly sophisticated. In fact, some businesses are forgoing regular websites altogether to focus on their Facebook page! My very basic Facebook page is at www.facebook.com/hcconsulting.

Since this section is meant as a high level overview, I'll outsource the mechanics of setting up a Facebook page to Facebook's own page creation site: http://www.facebook.com/pages/create.php. You may need to log into your Facebook personal profile first. Creating a basic page is fairly easy and straightforward. A great source of additional information on how to create compelling Facebook pages comes from a *PC World* article: http://bit.ly/PCWorldFBPg.

Once your page is set up, post content that is valuable to your target audience on the page status feed, and get people to follow you by "liking" your page (i.e. pressing the "Like" button). Successful Facebook pages can have thousands or millions of followers. By interspersing notices of your events or services within the helpful postings, you can generate additional revenue.

---

[6] Read about this in the Wall Street Journal (http://on.wsj.com/s8bKSj) and at Mashable (http://mashable.com/2011/08/01/authors-social-media/).

Twitter

Similarly, use Twitter to build a following 140 characters at a time. One of the ways to do this is to tweet useful links to those who could be your customers or clients, as if you were curating a reading list. *Google Reader* (page 54) makes it easy to quickly find interesting articles or blog posts that you would want to tweet to your followers.

Blogs

To successfully build a following with a blog, you have to write a post at least once a week (many bloggers post several times a day). Blogs can be time consuming to write. I have a blog on my website (www.hellmannconsulting.com/blog) but I update it a couple of times a month, not enough to build a following.

My blog has, however, served two business-building purposes despite these infrequent updates: 1) the information I provide in blog posts has been a valuable resource for clients and prospects, raising the profile of my website as a destination for people looking for the kind of help I can offer, and 2) I'm demonstrating expertise with my blog posts, which has helped to communicate value to potential purchasers of my services.

LinkedIn

LinkedIn is such a great tool for fostering *real* networking (relationships over time) that I would recommend continuing to use it to cultivate a network of people you know in some way (as discussed in the LinkedIn chapter). That is, don't try to build a following in LinkedIn by connecting with the whole world.

Instead, in addition to your LinkedIn profile and network, set up a LinkedIn "Company Page" to build followers. It's very easy to set up a company page. Simply select "Companies" from the top menu, then scroll to the right where you can click "Add a Company." After that, just follow the instructions to fill out the page.

As you set up your LinkedIn company page, you'll want to send status updates to your page followers, as you do with your Facebook page feed. To do that, in the Company Page Administration section, make sure you select "Designated Users Only" and then enter your name as the designated user.

To see the potential of a company page, check out *Deloitte's* company page by searching for it in the search box on the upper right (make sure "Companies" shows in the dropdown menu to the left of the search window).

I sometimes get asked whether someone should have two LinkedIn profiles (i.e. accounts), one for them personally and one for their business. The answer is no! As mentioned in the "LinkedIn" chapter, having more than one profile will ruin the power of LinkedIn as a networking tool.

Email Lists and other Online Groups

Email Lists, Yahoo Groups, LinkedIn Groups, and other specialty groups organized around a shared interest can be great for getting the word out to group members who could either buy your service directly or let others know about it. The key is to remember that the best groups are communities that are valued by the participants, where people help each other. So, be a resource to the other members! Don't overtly sell in these groups—you will be ostracized and quite possibly banned from the group if you are constantly hawking your "Seven Ways to…" book.

Instead, invest time in becoming a helpful presence within the group. Tactfully mention your service only on occasion and perhaps via a one-to-one message. Include a link to your product or service in the signature of your email or group posting. If you're pushy in a group, you will rightfully be pushed out.

Here are a couple of examples. I'm in a small specialty group for the contact management system I use. One of the regular posters, a source of useful help and information to the others, discreetly sells an email management service that is targeted to this audience. Over time, he has built up quite a positive reputation, as well as a substantial revenue stream, just from this little group.

Another colleague is co-president of a small startup company making affordable professional speakers for music enthusiasts and hobbyists. Virtually all their substantial revenue came initially from this kind of helpful, discreet, long-term participation in a forum for do-it-yourself recording artists.

Post to Several Applications at Once

Save time and have one posting go to all of your social media applications at once by posting via Hootsuite (www.hootsuite.com -- see Section 4 on Twitter) or another social media brand manager (e.g. Tweetdeck). For example, when I have something to share with followers, I will post it via Hootsuite to my Twitter feed, my LinkedIn profile-status-update, my Facebook page, and my Facebook personal profile all at the same time! For this to work, the post needs to be 140 characters maximum, since that's the maximum number of characters that Twitter allows.

How to Prioritize these Applications

When trying to build a following for your business, the priority you assign to each social media application may be different than what it is for a job search. That is, for many businesses, it's best to start with Facebook. The reason: Facebook usually has the most potential for building a following given its enormous base of very active users and its friendliness to posting via Hootsuite and other Social Media Managers. Posting discussions to a number of LinkedIn groups at once via Hootsuite (or something similar) can be very helpful to generating traffic to your website and interest in your profile. Twitter and blogs come next, then email lists.

The key rule to remember in prioritizing your social media efforts is to focus on the communication channels that are most likely to reach your customers. So, depending on your product or service, you might find a bigger or more receptive audience on LinkedIn or Twitter than on Facebook.

For example, if the market for your business-to-business technology solution includes Senior VPs of Information Technology, that audience may be more attuned to Twitter (it has a more hi-tech cachet) or LinkedIn (more "professional") than to Facebook. One-on-one outreach to sell your services to other executives and organizational decision-makers also may result in your prioritizing your LinkedIn network over building a following.

Guidelines for Posting to Followers

The general rule for social media postings: first quality (i.e. useful posts), then quantity. Here's what to say "yes" and "no" to:

YES: Postings of value, usually links to useful articles, discounts or advice that's really a value-add.

YES: Occasional announcements of your products or events: no more than one product reminder for every four helpful posts.

YES: Posting at least once a day, probably more.

YES: Throw in something personal every so often—so people can relate to you—especially if your business is you!

NO: Too many posts that no one cares about except for you and one other person.

NO: Relentless selling.

NO: Endless inspirational quotes.

How to Get Content for Your Posts

Google Reader or Hootsuite Columns can be used to quickly and easily curate information to share. To learn more about Google Reader, see Section 5, on Blogs. To learn about Hootsuite columns, see Section 4, on Twitter. Re-tweet interesting tweets that you capture in your Hootsuite columns to your followers not only on Twitter, but on LinkedIn and Facebook as well.

9. CROSS-PLATFORM THOUGHTS

"It takes many good deeds to build a good reputation, and one bad one to lose it."
Benjamin Franklin

Google Yourself

Type your name into Google and see what comes up (that's what many recruiters and hiring managers do). What do you find? Hopefully nothing bad; no embarrassing pictures from earlier days. When I google myself I find my career coaching website, my LinkedIn and Twitter profiles, my blog, an article I wrote, and an old website I created containing some music compositions. Phew, nothing embarrassing here! What if you don't like what comes up when you Google yourself? Here are a few suggestions:

- Un-tag yourself from embarrassing Facebook photos.
- Ask the host to take down the information.
- Restrict the privacy on your Facebook settings to your true "friends".
- Create your job-search profiles (e.g. LinkedIn, Twitter, Blogs, etc.) with a slightly different name (e.g. a middle initial, your maiden name) so they will not be connected to you.
- Put enough new information up on the web that the old, "bad" information gets buried.
- Do a search on the Internet for reputation "cleaners"—vet them carefully!
- Going forward, be careful about what you post on Facebook, etc. (including what you write) and monitor or restrict what others post about you.

Although a detailed review of how to protect and clean up your reputation is beyond the scope of this book, this subject is not to be taken lightly. A lot of information exists on the web about this topic if you need to know more: just enter "online reputation job search" in Google.

Mobile Applications ("Apps")

"There's an app for that" is pretty much the rule these days. If you own an iPhone, an Android Phone a Windows Phone or a Blackberry you'll find apps in each phone's "App Store" for all the social media tools in this book. But why bother with the download? It depends on the role you want your phone to play in your day-to-day productivity. For those who live on their phone, these apps can be very useful in keeping up with social media interactions.

It certainly can't hurt to download the free LinkedIn, Twitter Facebook, Wordpress, Hootsuite and Google apps and give them a try. I personally find the Google Reader app very useful for keeping up-to-date on the go.

APPENDIX 1: ADDITIONAL RESOURCES

General Career Management

www.hellmannconsulting.com : **Hellmann Career Consulting**, the website for my career coaching practice. On this site, you'll find:

- The archive for my Career blog, which offers advice on a range issues spanning the job search, career change, and success on the job.
- A Career Links page, with all links tested by me. Use these links for essential job target research.
- A Seminars page which lists seminars and webinars (some of them recorded) on the job search and career management that I lead, most of which are open to the public.

www.fiveoclockclub.com **: The Five O'Clock Club's** job search methodology has been referenced repeatedly in this book, and is second to none. On this site you'll find a variety of career resources as well as the ability to join their fee-based weekly job search groups.

Resources that Help You Use Twitter

Twitter is not just a self-contained platform like LinkedIn. In order to use it most effectively, you need to go outside of Twitter to the numerous external applications and Twitter directories on the web. Here's a sample listing.

- Popular Social Media Dashboards include (there are many others):
    - www.hootsuite.com
    - www.tweetdeck.com
    - www.bufferapp.com
    - www.twimbow.com
- www.socialoomph.com : this site allows you to extend Twitter's features.
- A guide to Twitter Acronyms: http://www.labnol.org/internet/popular-twitter-acronyms/6819/
- Free Twitter background template, to improve your professional appearance: http://theclosetentrepreneur.com/create-a-twitter-background-using-powerpoint
- A resource guide to Twitter: http://www.twitip.com/
- http://www.careerrocketeer.com/2009/09/top-100-job-search-hashtags-on-twitter.html for other example hashtags.
- Find people to follow by using **directories** of people who tweet.
    - www.wefollow.com sorts tweeps by interest, then ranks them by a "prominence" score.
    - www.twellow.com : broken out by industry/profession.
    - www.tweetstork.com : find users based on their description.

- o www.justtweetit.com : find people who share your interests.
  - o www.followerwonk.com : Identifies tweeps by keyword, then ranks them by their proprietary "Social Authority" score.
- Search Twitter Job Postings.
  - o Twitter Job Search: http://www.twitjobsearch.com/ type in "Marketing Manager in New York." Notice the hashtags. May give you ideas for other tags to follow.
  - o http://jobmob.co.il/blog/twitter-job-openings-postings-leads/ List of Twitter job feeds globally, by type of industry/profession.
  - o http://twitter.com/jobshouts filter using keywords.

Sites that Facilitate Social Media Posting

These sites do things like allow you to post in one place to multiple social media sites, view all your social media activity from one portal, shorten URLs, and so forth.

- www.hootsuite.com
- www.tweetdeck.com
- www.bufferapp.com
- www.onlywire.com Allows posting to 52 different social networks (e.g. LinkedIn, Twitter, Facebook, etc.). $12.99/month.
- http://www.linksalpha.com/ : enables you to publish to multiple social media applications (inexpensive)
- http://bit.ly/ : URL shortener.
- http://ow.ly/url/shorten-url : URL shortener.

Articles and how-to's on Social Media

www.mashable.com

Other Online Social Media Sites

www.foursquare.com : Popular with companies building their "brick & mortar" business and brand.

www.google.com/+ : Google+, Google's answer to Facebook. The verdict is generally accepted to be still out on the ultimate success of this new platform.

www.yahoogroups.com : If you can find the right group, this portal could be very helpful in learning about your target. Yahoo groups are more like email lists than LinkedIn groups.

www.pinterest.com : Pinterest is a personalized media platform with a huge social component. Users can manage images and other media (i.e. videos) through collections. Very popular now with those who have something "visual" to say.

APPENDIX 2: EIGHT RULES FOR WRITING GREAT LETTERS

Every so often I hear the comment that "nobody reads cover letters." That's because most of the letters jobseekers send are just too hard to get through! Follow these rules and not only will your letter be read, but you'll greatly improve the odds of getting the result you want.

Rule #1: Make your letter easily "scannable"
These days, work is too fast-paced to allow for reading through a long, dense letter. DON'T take a page out of your English Literature 101 class. Instead, make your letter a quick, easy read by:

- Using short paragraphs– no more than seven lines in any one paragraph (assuming an 8.5×11 Word document). Less than seven lines is better.
- Using bullet points (e.g. like this).
- Using bold-face and/or <u>underlining</u> of key phrases to bring them out. Make sure you use this technique sparingly– if too much is in bold or underlined, it will defeat the purpose and look terrible.
- Considering the use of sub-headings. This blog post, with its use of the "rules" subheadings, is an example.
- Minimizing repetition. You don't need to mention your extensive marketing background three times– once is enough. So make sure you minimize repetition.

Rule #2: Default to using email
Start with the presumption that you are going to write your letter of introduction, cover letter, or interview/meeting follow-up as an email, then "convince yourself" why using postal mail would be better. The reasons you want to default to email: first, it works (as I see every day with clients), and second, sending an email is so much faster. You can skip finding/buying stamps, getting the envelope to print properly, and remembering to mail the letter (it usually takes me about three days!). The table below summarizes the pros and cons of sending an email vs. mailing a letter.

Email vs. Postal Mail in a Job Search: Pros vs. Cons

Email		Letter by Postal Mail	
✓	Fast for you	X	Time consuming
✓	Easy to respond	X	Hard to respond
✓	Everyone reads email	X	Delay in getting/reading mail
✓	Quick Delivery	X	Longer Delivery
✓	It works!	✓	It works!
X	Spam Issues	✓	No Spam Issues
X	Just another email	✓	Stands Out
❖	More Current	❖	More Old School
❖ symbol means "pros/cons depend on the recipient"			

Your job search time is valuable. Perhaps you've heard of the expression "the perfect is the enemy of the good." There's so much that you need to do in a job search, so go for "good" or even "great" in your search and let go of "perfect."

That said, there are several situations where sending a letter by mail will get you a better result.

1. If you've had an informational or networking meeting and someone really helped you, a handwritten note of appreciation is a very nice touch!
2. If you feel the person to whom you are reaching out is more "old school," e.g. from an older generation, more conservative, etc. then a letter may be more appropriate.
3. A letter will stand out more than an email will, improving the odds of it being read. To help a letter stand out even more, consider sending it by "Priority Mail." If you have the time, you could send an email and, if no response, then a letter.

Rule #3: Always include the "letter" in the body of the email, as people don't like to open attachments. Enough said.

Rule #4: Engage them with the Email Subject Line
If you do use email, the subject line is key to your message being read. Don't make it too salesy or pushy. Mention something that they are interested in so that your email gets opened! Examples include:

- "Your article about Supply Chain in…"
- "Referred by Susan Smith, re:…"
- "Open to discussing Fundraising at Ivy University?"
- "Our three mutual connections and shared group on LinkedIn"
- "Hello, and question…" <if you know them>

Rule #5: Make sure your email address is professional

doggie23@hotmail.com won't cut it. firstnamelastname@gmail.com will make a better impression and make you more likely to get past the spam filters.

Rule #6: Focus on them

I get so many drafts that are all about "me me me" when the tone/language should be "here's how I can help you…" , "I believe this meeting would be mutually beneficial because…" or "Your company's Vision resonates…" If you want them to help you, show appreciation, as in "I would greatly appreciate…" A simple "thank you" can of course go a long way. Sounds easy and obvious but too many clients forget these basic rules of relationships.

Rule #7: Include your pitch (if you haven't in a prior letter)

Inform the people to whom you are writing of your background and link it to how you can help them. Summarize your background in one or two sentences, and then share some relevant background highlights by including three to six "bulleted" accomplishments. Don't assume that even your best, closest work colleague knows how you want to position yourself, or remembers the great things you've done. Also, strangers will naturally want to know from whom they are hearing. A powerful pitch in your email can really help to illustrate how you can help an organization, engage the reader, and spur the action you want.

Rule #8: End with a clear call to action

Say "Would you have 20 minutes available on your calendar to meet?" (it's so easy for them to hit reply on an email and say yes.) And/or, say "I'll contact your office to see if I can get on your calendar in a few days, assuming I don't hear from you first."

I'll be posting more in the near future about how to write great email content that gets you the meetings you want, as well has how to follow up with a phone call.

GLOSSARY OF TERMS

@username: (Twitter) the @ sign signifies the Twitter name of the person. For me it would be @robhellmann. So, you might see "RT @robhellmann:" followed by the tweet content.

1st Degree Network: (LinkedIn) The people you connect with directly.

2nd Degree Network: (LinkedIn) The people who connect directly with your 1st degree network.

3rd Degree Network: (LinkedIn) The people who connect directly with your 2nd degree network.

Blog: "a type of website, usually maintained by an individual with regular entries of commentary, descriptions of events, or other material such as graphics or video." (Wikipedia)

Email Lists: (also referred to as electronic mailing lists) Messages among individuals who subscribe to the list that form conversations around specific topics. These conversations can be archived and are searchable.

Facebook: A social media application that allows users to add people as "friends," in order to send them messages and updates on their personal profiles. Additionally, users can join networks organized by workplace, school, or profession.

Feed: (Twitter) a stream of all the tweets you have received or sent.

Group: LinkedIn members who congregate in an organized LinkedIn forum around a specific topic, profession, or association.

Hashtags: (Twitter) These reference the "#" character, as in #jobs, #marketing, etc. They signify user-created topics that catch on with a lot of users, and become conventions for searching by topic.

Job Board: Websites that contain online ads for job openings. www.indeed.com is one such job board, and there are many others. Go to the links page on my website (scroll down) to see more.

Keyword: (Twitter) a stream of tweets based on an individual keyword search.

Link Shorteners: (Twitter) since tweets are no longer than 140 characters, link shrinking is essential. Most Twitter organizers can shrink your links for you if you enter the full link on the top of the screen (where you would tweet) and click "Shrink It." Online services such as http://ow.ly/url/shorten-url can also shrink your links for you.

LinkedIn: a service accessed at www.linkedin.com that enables users to keep in touch with and expand their professional network, get introductions to others outside their immediate network, and join groups of professionals organized around industries, professions, and associations.

Lists stream: a Twitter organizer column that contains a public Twitter list you are following, or a list of tweeters that you are compiling yourself (public or private).

Lists: Compiled by Twitter users (anyone can create a public or private list), and aggregate people tweeting on a particular topic. The advantage of lists is that you can get all the tweets at once from individuals on the list—you don't have to follow each individual.

Networking: Building and maintaining relationships over time that can lead to interviews or referrals.

Pitch (or elevator speech): a concise statement about how you would be valuable to an employer.

RT (re-tweet): (Twitter) a convention for "re-tweet." If you are passing on the information from someone else's tweet, it is common courtesy to add RT, and the username, within the tweet you are forwarding (that is, re-tweeting).

Search columns: (Twitter) Search columns allow searching by phrases, using connections such as "And," "Or," and so forth.

Social Media: Primarily online or mobile media that enables conversation and interaction between people.

Social Media Dashboard: Organizes social media posts that you are monitoring, from different platforms (e.g. Twitter, Facebook, LinkedIn, etc.) into columns, or "filing cabinets." Enables you to post to multiple platforms from one place. Hootsuite is a popular example.

Stream: (Twitter) a column of tweets (or posts from other applications) in Hootsuite that is generated by search terms or the name of a Twitter list.

All tweets in Hootsuite are separated into individual streams/columns.

Tab: (Twitter) a category on Hootsuite that contains up to 10 streams (or columns).

Tweep: (Twitter) a follower on Twitter.

Twitter: a free service at www.twitter.com that enables its users to send and read messages known as tweets. These are messages of up to 140 characters that are displayed on the author's profile page and delivered to the author's subscribers who are known as followers. All users can send and receive tweets via the Twitter website or external applications.

Word cloud: enables you to visually see the frequency of words that show up in a block of text. If you google "Word Cloud" you will see the many free tools that can enable you to create word clouds. I use "TagCrowd" at www.tagcrowd.com. Word clouds are helpful in identifying keywords for your resume or LinkedIn profile.

Your purchase of this book entitles you to download the digital eBook for this edition, for free!

To download the book, follow these steps.

1. Go to the "book" page of my website:
   http://hellmannconsulting.com/book

2. Click the "Buy" button for the eBook.

3. Enter "**paperback**" in the discount window (without the quotes).

4. Click "update cart," then "checkout."

NOTES PAGE

NOTES PAGE

.

Made in the USA
Lexington, KY
13 January 2014